PHILOSOPHICAL ESSAYS

A CRITICAL EDITION

Fernando Pessoa

Selected Other Works by Fernando Pessoa

Mensagem

Tales of a Reasoner

The Book of Disquietude

The Keeper of Sheep

The Education of the Stoic

PHILOSOPHICAL ESSAYS

A CRITICAL EDITION

Fernando Pessoa

EDITION, NOTES, & INTRODUCTION
Nuno Ribeiro

AFTERWORD
Paulo Borges

Contra Mundum Press   New York

Philosophical Essays: A Critical Edition © 2012 by Nuno Ribeiro
Afterword © 2012 Paulo Borges

First Contra Mundum Press edition 2012. The main text of this edition is a transcription of material from the Fernando Pessoa Archive catalogued at the Biblioteca Nacional de Portugal: E3 (Espólio 3: 3rd Archive).

All Rights Reserved under International & Pan-American Copyright Conventions. No part of this book may be reproduced in any form or by any electronic means, including information storage and retrieval systems, without permission in writing from the publisher, except by a reviewer who may quote brief passages in a review.

Library of Congress Cataloguing-in-Publication Data

Pessoa, Fernando, 1888–1935

[Philosophical Essays. A Critical Edition. English.]
Philosophical Essays: A Critical Edition / Fernando Pessoa

—1st Contra Mundum Press Edition
260 pp., 5x8 in.

ISBN 9780983697268

   I. Pessoa, Fernando.
  II. Title.
 III. Ribeiro, Nuno.
 IV. Introduction.
  V. Borges, Paulo.
 VI. Afterword.

2012953735

TABLE OF CONTENTS

Introduction — Nuno Ribeiro 0

PART I. PHILOSOPHICAL ESSAYS

I — Essay on the Nature and Meaning of Rationalism (Unsigned) 2

II — Essay on Free-Will (Charles Robert Anon) 26
   A) Projects 26
   B) Fragments 28

III — On the Idea of Responsibility (Unsigned) 80

IV — Essay on the Idea of Cause (Alexander Search) 92

V — On Error (Unsigned) 98

VI — On Sensation (Unsigned) 104

VII — Essay on Heraclitus (Unsigned) 114

VIII — On Thomas Aquinas (Unsigned) 128

IX — Essay on Pascal (Unsigned) 134

X — On the Limits of Science (Charles Robert Anon) 138

PART II. ADDENDA

1 — Further Writings concerning Rationalism 142

1.1 — Preliminary Sketches for the "Essay on the Nature and Meaning of Rationalism" 142

    A) 1st Stage (Unsigned) 142

    B) 2nd Stage (Unsigned) 147

1.2 — An Examination of Rationalism (Unsigned) 154

2 — Further Writings concerning Free-Will 160

2.1 — Against the Death Penalty (Unsigned) 160

2.2 — Essay on Liberty (Unsigned) 163

    A) Projects 163

    B) Fragments 165

3 — Fragments with References to the Idea of Cause (Charles Robert Anon) 169

    From the Notebook of Charles Robert Anon 172

4 — Fragments with References to the Concept of Sensation (Unsigned) 174

Afterword — Paulo Borges 180

Bibliography 188

INTRODUCTION

1

PESSOA'S ENGLISH EDUCATION

The Portuguese poet and thinker Fernando Pessoa was born in Lisbon on June 13, 1888, to Maria Magdalena Pinheiro Nogueira & Joaquim de Seabra Pessoa. Pessoa's father died of tuberculosis on July 13, 1893, when Pessoa was five years old, and in December 1895, Pessoa's mother married João Miguel Rosa. The trajectory of Pessoa's life changed drastically in January 1896, when Rosa moved the new family to Durban, South Africa, where he began to serve as the Portuguese consul. As a result of his stepfather's position, Pessoa grew up in South Africa and had an English education. This would deeply affect his mature literary production, much of which was written in English.

Pessoa first attended St. Joseph's in Durban, a convent school run by Dominican Sisters, and was transferred to Durban High School in April 1899, where he studied for the next three years (see image next page).

INTRODUCTION

28A-2

Durban High School Record.

Year _____
[To be filled in at Editorial Office

DETAILS FOR THE SCHOOL ROLL

You are earnestly requested to fill in this form and return it at your earliest convenience to—

G. O. COLLINS, COMMERCE COURT, DURBAN.

Please add the names and addresses of any of your contemporaries or other O.B.'s whom you know. The Editors desire to impress upon Old Boys that owing to the Incomplete state of the School Registers, the most cordial co-operation of correspondents is necessary in order that the "Record" may be of real value. Old Boys who have not been communicated with previously are informed that the "D.H.S. Record" will be published about May, 1905, and will form a complete (and profusely illustrated) history of the School. There will be about 200 pp. of letterpress and the volume will be bound in full leather. Copies may be ordered, price £1 1s. each (payable on delivery) from the Publishers, Messrs. JOHN SINGLETON & SONS, West Street, Durban. A list of Subscribers will be published with the book.

NAME (in full).	Fernando Antonio Nogueira Pessôa.
YEAR OF ENTRY.	First time, April, 1899; second time, February, 1904.
YEAR OF DEPARTURE.	First time, June, 1901; second time, December, 19..
HOUSE. *The "House" system was introduced in April, 1902. Old Boys before that date will please state simply "Day-Boy" or "Boarder."*	When I was first at School there were no houses; the second time, I was in Ballance's House.
ADDRESS.	P.O. Box 315, Durban.
SCHOOL CAREER. [Under this heading please state what forms you were in, what exams. you passed, School prizes secured, whether you were a Bursar, Exhibitions, etc. Also any "House" or School colours secured, your best athletic performances, etc. Give details where possible.]	I entered into Form II.B, passed in June into II.A, a year after (June 1900) into the third Form. After six months I was put into the IV. which I left on first date of departure abovementioned. From return to my definite departure I was in the VI. I passed the Cape School Higher Examination, in first class, in June 1901, and in December 1904, Cape Intermediate, in the Second Class. I got three school prizes: a Form Prize in Form II.A (Dec 1899), VI. (June 1904) and a French Prize in the III. Form.
SUBSEQUENT CAREER. [Under this heading please state your subsequent school (if any) and University; your Professional or Commercial successes and your athletic performances. Also your present occupation, Municipal Colonial or Imperial Honours, whether married (if so, to whom and date), whether in the Militia (if so, name of corps, rank and service). Any other details (e.g. list of publications) will be welcomed.]	

[BNP/E3, 28a–20^r]

er this heading please state—
1. Names and addresses of any other O.B.'s
2. Any interesting incident connected with the School or the Colony which you may remember. These will be useful for the Chapters of School reminiscences.

In 1901, Pessoa passed the Cape School Higher Examination with distinction, and in August of the same year embarked for Portugal with his family, where they remained for a year. When Pessoa returned to South Africa in September 1902, he was enrolled in the Durban Commercial School, and then in 1903 he applied to the University of the Cape of Good Hope. Pessoa's marks on the Matriculation Examination were unimpressive, but he was nevertheless awarded — of 899 candidates — a Queen Victoria Memorial Prize for the best essay in English. When he later took the Intermediate Examination at the University of the Cape of Good Hope, in 1904, he obtained the highest results of all the regional candidates from Natal, South Africa. Pessoa's marks on the Intermediate Examination entitled him to a scholarship to study in England, but the scholarship had a condition: recipients had to have studied in South Africa for the three previous years. Since Pessoa's return to Portugal in 1901–1902 had interrupted his residency, he was deemed ineligible. With England ruled out, Pessoa decided to definitively return to Portugal, where he enrolled in the Curso Superior de Letras (Superior

Course of Letters) at the University of Lisbon. Pessoa attended philosophy classes in 1906 & 1907, and it was during this early period in Lisbon that he elaborated his projects for philosophical works. In South Africa, he had primarily been concerned with literary and poetic projects, so the Lisbon years constitute a turning point: they are characterized by Pessoa's emphasis on philosophical research and his interest in penning philosophical works. During these Lisbon years, he outlined many philosophical essays in English, while his interest in philosophy and philosophical projects later appears to diminish.

But throughout his life, Pessoa never abandoned the idea of writing in English. His first literary experiments were published in English, in the South African *Natal Mercury* — including a poem he signed as Charles Robert Anon. This reveals that Pessoa's practice of writing under other names originates in his youth, as I will discuss in more detail below. After his return to Portugal, Pessoa continues to write in English — as mature texts like "Antinous" and *35 Sonnets* both demonstrate. Above all, however, it is Pessoa's philosophical essays & project drafts that reflect his lasting interest in writing in English. All of the pieces in this volume were originally composed in English, and this is one aspect of their significance. Given a global interest in the philosophical subtlety of Pessoa's poetry, the publication of his English philosophical essays should provoke no less interest.

Prominent international philosophers like Alain Badiou and Simon Critchley have worked on Pessoa's poetry, while Portuguese intellectuals have likewise treated Pessoa as a philosophical provocateur.[1] In the wake of classic works such as José Gil's *Fernando Pessoa ou la métaphysique des sensations*, Eduardo Lourenço's *Fernando Pessoa, Roi de notre Bavière*, and Paulo Borges' *O Teatro da Vacuidade ou a impossibilidade de ser eu*, a new generation of Portuguese and international researchers are engaged in philosophical investigations of Pessoa's work, too.[2] The present edition can serve as an illuminating guide for future work on Pessoa's relationship to philosophy.

---

1. See the chapter "A Philosophical Task: To Be Contemporaries of Pessoa" in Alain Badiou, *Handbook of Inaesthetics* (California: Stanford University Press, 2005) 36–45, and Simon Critchley, "Surfaciality: Some Poems by Fernando Pessoa, one by Wallace Stevens, and the Brief Sketch of a Poetic Ontology," *Gramma*, v. 14 (2006) 107–130.
2. For example, see the volume edited by Paulo Borges entitled *Olhares Europeus sobre Fernando Pessoa* (Lisbon: Centro de Filosofia da Universidade de Lisboa, 2010), which contains essays by Portuguese, Spanish, German, and Italian thinkers.

2
THE PESSOA ARCHIVE AND THE UNPUBLISHED PHILOSOPHICAL WRITINGS

In 1905, the year Pessoa returned to Portugal, he began a long and intense period of literary creation that lasted until his death in 1935, though most of this work remained unknown during his life. In fact, Pessoa published only one book while he was alive, *Mensagem* (*Message*), which was released the year before his death. Aside from *Mensagem*, he also published poems and articles in a variety of literary journals and magazines, but those texts did not constitute a book. Rather, they were generally conceived as parts of other books — books that were to come — as he asserts in many of his letters.

In the Pessoa Archive, which is housed in the Biblioteca Nacional de Portugal (BNP), one finds outlines for a host of projects as well as fragments Pessoa wrote in Portuguese, English, and French on the most diverse topics. Besides his poetry and fiction, Pessoa delves into politics and economics, mysticism and astrology. These unpublished writings have provided the grist for a number of philological, literary, and philosophical studies since Pessoa's death, and still give rise to disagreement over how best to publish them. Among Pessoa's unpublished projects, one finds the *Philosophical Essays* — the material that comprises this volume.

Although some of the texts presented here have been published previously,[3] most of them are being published here for the first time, while this edition is novel in other regards. To date, the only other edition to be exclusively concerned with Pessoa's philosophical writings is António Pina Coelho's *Textos Filosóficos de Fernando Pessoa*,[4] which was first printed in 1968, and which suffers from a series of problems. To begin with, it contains only a limited selection of Pessoa's philosophical texts — mainly those that are easiest to transcribe — while Coelho restricts himself to just four of the Pessoa Archive's fourteen philosophical envelopes. Moreover, Coelho's selection, transcription, & organization of Pessoa's texts follow no critical criteria. Texts are ranged according to thematic concepts that correspond neither to any thematic principle established by Pessoa, nor to any project conceived by Pessoa for distributing these texts. In effect, Coelho presents the various *Textos Filosóficos* as if they were loose sheets, lacking any discernible connection among themselves. Perhaps due to this, his edition failed to evoke any serious interest in Pessoa's philosophical writings.[5]

---

3. It is impossible to state exactly the precise number of unpublished texts considering the amount of articles and books concerning new aspects of the Pessoa Archive that have been and are currently being published. As a reference, we follow the main editions of Pessoa's work.

4. Fernando Pessoa, *Textos Filosóficos de Fernando Pessoa*, ed. with a preface by António Pina Coelho (Lisbon: Ática, 1968).

Two other volumes related to this material include Pedro Teixeira da Mota's *Fernando Pessoa. Moral, Regras de Vida, Condições de Iniciação*, and Teresa Rita Lopes' *Pessoa Inédito*.⁶ Mota's book contains a selection of philosophical writings that concern moral problems — notably, some projects for Pessoa's "Essay on Free-Will." But his edition is only partially devoted to philosophical texts; it also contains mystical & ritual texts by Pessoa, as well as literary texts that are not directly linked to his philosophical efforts. Moreover, Mota's selection — like Coelho's — follows no principle or project established by Pessoa. In Lopes's edition, on the other hand, there is only one chapter devoted to

---

5. In some recent articles I analyze in detail the problems concerned with the earlier edition of Coelho's *Textos Filosoficos*. See: Nuno Ribeiro, "Os Livro Filosóficos Inacabados de Pessoa — Problemas e Critérios para a Publicação dos Escritos Filosóficos de Pessoa," *Philosophica*, Nº 38 (Lisbon: Edições Colibri, 2011) 165 – 174; Nuno Ribeiro, "Tive em mim milhares de Filosofias" — questões para a edição dos escritos filosóficos inéditos de Pessoa," *cultura* ENTRE *culturas*, Nº 3 (Lisbon: Âncora Editora, 2011) 192 – 200. In the second volume of my doctoral dissertation, I present an alternative and more complete edition of Pessoa's philosophical writings: Nuno Ribeiro, *Tradição e Pluralismo nos Escritos Filosóficos de Fernando Pessoa* & *Escritos Filosóficos de Fernando Pessoa* (Lisbon: Faculdade de Ciências Sociais e Humanas da Universidade Nova de Lisboa, 2012).
6. Teresa Rita Lopes (ed.), *Pessoa Inédito* (Lisbon: Livros Horizonte, 1993) see specifically pages 106 – 109 (2.13. "Onde o poeta se manifesta animado pela filosofia") and 397 – 420 (8. "Um poeta animado pela Filosofia").

philosophical texts, yet it also contains a number of non-philosophical texts by Pessoa.[7]

The novelty of the present edition, then, is not only that it presents hitherto unpublished — and in many cases, previously unknown — philosophical writings by Pessoa, but also that these texts are arranged in light of the philosophical projects conceived by Pessoa himself. As scrupulously as possible, this edition presents Pessoa's philosophical fragments in the order and structure that Pessoa started to realize, but never finished — and under the several names he signed them with.

In a draft, Pessoa once writes out the title *Philosophical Essays* (see image on XII), without entirely specifying which of his essays should be included under that title.[8]

---

7. Besides the problematic editions of Pessoa's philosophical texts, and the two texts mentioned above, there are also sporadic references to the philosophical texts in other books on Pessoa. For one example, see Pablo Javier Pérez López's *Poesía, Ontología y Tragedia en Fernando Pessoa*. But López's book presents the same problems as Coelho's (which is used as one of the bases for the analysis of Pessoa's philosophy).

8. This draft (written circa 1906–1907) is in the Pessoa Archive. In it, Pessoa outlines a list of essays, all of which he scratched out; in place of those titles he wrote "Philosophical Essays," thereby indicating a sketch of a new list, but without accurately denoting which essays were to be included in the proposed book, revealing a lack of clarity (or decision) about the contents. In fact, throughout the Pessoa Archive, one finds hundreds of projects and lists of works, most of which Pessoa abandoned. This list, although representative of his interest in gathering many of his essays under the title "Philosophical Essays," is very confusing and unclear.

But the Pessoa Archive preserves many fragments for philosophical essays, and I believe that there is no more accurate title under which to gather these fragments. The present edition collects what was produced (and has

---

It contains, for instance, in the scratched out list, references to "studies in phrenology, physiognomy, etc.," as well as "The study of the character," which Pessoa very specifically classifies, in another document, as "Microsophy" [BNP/E3, 24-120ᵛ], not as philosophy. In that definition of Microsophy, Pessoa lists five categories distinctly not related to philosophy:

Microsophy = the science of the minute.

Includes:
- 1. Phrenology.
- 2. Physiognomy.
- 3. Graphology.
- 4. Childology.
- 5. All other small sciences.

[BNP/E3, 24-120ᵛ]

The scratched out list also contains "spiritualism" as an entry, but that should be considered in the context of Pessoa's esoteric thought, which constitutes an entirely different area of the archive. In fact, most of the titles concerning esotericism will appear in other lists not marked "Philosophical Essays." Therefore, in general, the list is not representative of the philosophical activity developed by Pessoa concerning the writing of the "Philosophical Essays." That is a possible reason for Pessoa's scratching out the first list and not completing the second, hoping perhaps to develop a superior (or simply definitive and final) list in the future, but he never writes such a list. The title serves then only as an indication of the plan for gathering many of his philosophical texts under the designation "Philosophical Essays."

survived) of Pessoa's English *Philosophical Essays* — that is to say, the fragments of a collection that he never himself finished.

[BNP/E3, 48B-152ʳ]

3

PHILOSOPHY IN THE CONTEXT OF PESSOA'S WORK

Many have noticed that Pessoa refers to philosophers and philosophical concepts throughout his literary oeuvre. What is still scarcely known is the extent to which his interest in philosophy outstrips these references. In an autobiographical English text concerning his poetical production, Pessoa writes:

> I was a poet animated by philosophy, not a philosopher with poetic faculties. I loved to admire the beauty of things, to trace in the imperceptible and w through the minute the poetic soul of the universe.

> I was a poet animated by philosophy
> not a philosopher with poetic facul-
> ties. I loved to admire the beauty of
> things, to trace in the impercept-
> ible and through the minute the poetic
> soul of the universe.
>
> The poetry of the earth is never dead.
> We may say that ages gone have been
> more poetic, but we can say
>
> Poetry is in everything — in land
> and in sea, in lake and in river

[BNP/E3, 20-11ʳ]

This text, which is often used by Pessoa scholars to provide proof of his interest in philosophy, can be only considered as partially true — like most of his 'autobiographical' statements. If we observe the number of philosophical concepts that recur throughout his poetic, literary, and fictional creations, there is sufficient support for the truth of this statement. And yet: it was *not* only through poetic, literary, and fictional creations — that is to say, as "a poet" — that Pessoa expressed his interest in philosophy. Besides his being "a poet animated by philosophy," one finds proof in the Pessoa Archive that he was also the author of a series of straightforwardly *philosophical* prose pieces that remained unpublished during his lifetime.

The Pessoa Archive, which is catalogued at the Biblioteca Nacional de Portugal (BNP) under the designation E3 (Espólio 3: 3rd Archive), is divided into envelopes and comprises more than 27,000 sheets *in toto*. Each envelope is classified by a number & a designation, and holds a varying number of sheets. Among these many envelopes, 14 are devoted to philosophy, and they contain a total of 1,428 separate sheets — a testament to Pessoa's philosophical output.[9] To give a single example, on a fragment whose verso is signed by Alexander Search — an English pre-heteronym of Pessoa's — one reads:

> Thousands of theories, grotesque, extraordinary, profound, on the world, on man, on all problems that pertain to metaphysics have passed through my mind. I have had in me thousands of philosophies not any two of which — as if they were real — agreed. All the ideas I had if written down had been a great cheque on posterity; but by the very peculiar character of my mind, no sooner did the theory, the idea strike me that it disappeared, and after I ached to feel that one moment after I remembered nothing — absolutely nothing of what it might have been. Thus memory, as all my other faculties predisposed me to live in a dream.

---

9. There are five envelopes (15^1, 15^2, 15^3, 15^4, and 15^5) with the designation "Filosofia," one (15A) with "Filosofia-Metafísica," four ($15B^1$, $15B^2$, $15B^3$, and $15B^4$) with "Filosofia-Psicologia" and, finally, four (22, 23, 24, and 25) with "Textos Filosóficos."

[BNP/E3, 15B³-12]

Aside from English texts, the archive also contains texts written in Portuguese and French that touch on figures of the philosophical tradition and that explore philosophical concepts. These texts, which were typically conceived as being part of larger projects, are also unfinished. The fragmentary character of Pessoa's philosophical writings is consistent with what we find elsewhere in the archive, and he gives an account of this incompleteness in the following English text:

> My writings were none of them finished; new thoughts intruded ever, extraordinary, inexcusable associations of ideas bearing infinity for term. I cannot prevent my thoughts hatred of finish[ing]; [...]

> My character of mind is such that I hate the beginnings
> and the ends of things, for they are definite points.[10]

Thus, Pessoa's philosophical fragments express the unfinished character of his writings in general. The Pessoa Archive preserves over 1,000 of the most diverse kind of philosophical texts by Pessoa — on the concepts of sensation, free-will, causality, & so on — while among them one finds the elements of Pessoa's *Philosophical Essays*.

Pessoa's *Philosophical Essays* date from, or were at least begun during the 1906–1907 Lisbon period. On the whole, the texts were attributed to two English literary personalities that Pessoa had invented in South Africa: Charles Robert Anon and Alexander Search. These pre-heteronyms are independent literary personalities with complex biographies and literary works of their own, and in these pre-heteronymic personalities, we can see the first clear indications of Pessoa's later, much-discussed "heteronyms."

In a "Bibliographical Notice" he published in 1928 in a Portuguese literary review, *Presença*, Pessoa introduced Alberto Caeiro, Ricardo Reis, and Álvaro de Campos as his only heteronyms (to date). While Pessoa does not say in that text whether or not he will publish under other heteronyms in the future, he does give us

---

10. Fernando Pessoa, *Escritos Autobiográficos, Automáticos e de Reflexão Pessoal* (Lisbon: Assírio & Alvim, 2003) 100.

some clues for understanding his notion of a "heteronym." In the text, Pessoa makes this differentiation between a heteronym and a pseudonym: "The pseudonym's work is the work of the author in its own person, save the name he signs; the heteronym's work is the work of the author outside its own person."[11] In a text titled "Aspects," which was supposed to serve as an introduction to his heteronymic works, he explains further:

> You should approach these books as if you hadn't read this explanation but had simply read the books, buying them one by one at a bookstore, where you saw them on display. You shouldn't read them in any other spirit. [...] That doesn't mean you have the right to believe in my explanation. As soon as you read it, you should suppose that I've lied — that you're going to read books by different poets, or different writers, and that through those books you'll receive emotions and learn lessons from those writers, with whom I have nothing to do except as their publisher.[12]

Pessoa produces an array of texts written in different styles and attributed to a catalogue of heteronyms. By

---

11. "A obra pseudónyma é do autor em sua pessoa, salvo o nome que assina; a heterónyma é do auctor fora da sua pessoa." Fernando Pessoa, "Tábua Bibliográfica," *Presença*, nº 17 (1928) 10.
12. Fernando Pessoa, *Selected Prose of Fernando Pessoa*, ed. and tr. by Richard Zenith (New York: Grove Press, 2001) 4-5.

doing so, he becomes a plurality of literary personalities, each of whom has authored "works." Two examples of his heteronymic work are *The Keeper of Sheep*, written under the name of Alberto Caeiro, and *Book of Odes*, written in a Horatian style, under the name of Ricardo Reis. Pessoa's plurality of heteronyms expresses his conception of the self as a multiplicity. Throughout the works of Pessoa's heteronyms, one finds traces of this conception of a decentered self that was, most probably, inspired by Nietzsche.[13] In the poetry of the heteronym Ricardo Reis, one reads: "Countless lives inhabit us."[14] In the poem "Passage of Time," the heteronym Álvaro de Campos says of himself: "I'm more varied than a random crowd, / I'm more diverse than the spontaneous universe."[15] In poem XXIX of *The Keeper of Sheep*, Caeiro, the most desubjectivated of all of the heteronyms, affirms: "I'm not always the same in what I say and write."[16] The poetry & prose of 'Pessoa' is rife with statements of this kind.

---

13. In my book *Fernando Pessoa e Nietzsche: O pensamento da pluralidade*, I outline in detail the connection between Nietzsche's view of the self as a multiplicity and the construction of the heteronomy in Pessoa's work, developing, just as well, a genealogy of the concept of the heteronym from Nietzsche's perspectivalism.
14. Fernando Pessoa, *Fernando Pessoa & Co.* (New York: Grove Press, 1998) 137.
15. Álvaro de Campos, *Poesia*, ed. by Teresa Rita Lopes (Lisbon: Companhia das Letras, 2002) 244.
16. Alberto Caeiro, *Poesia*, ed. by Fernando Cabral Martins (Lisbon: Assírio & Alvim, 2001).

But Pessoa's creation of a pluralist 'Pessoa' has a branching, convoluted structure. Besides the heteronyms, one finds other literary personalities in his oeuvre. If we may speak of his heteronym as a literary personality, then we can also say that a heteronym is only *one* such personality, and that he creates others — the semi-heteronym, sub-heteronym, and pre-heteronym. Or put differently, if 'literary personality' can be conceived as a genus, then Pessoa's heteronyms, semi-heteronyms, sub-heteronyms, and pre-heteronyms can be regarded as its species. And all of these types of literary personalities help to structure his literary space.

Pessoa's oeuvre includes a number of works by semi-heteronyms — take *The Book of Disquiet* by Bernardo Soares, or *The Education of the Stoic* by the Baron of Teive — as well as a set of texts by sub-heteronyms like Thomas Crosse and I.I. Crosse. The difference between a heteronym and a semi-heteronym is this: a heteronym differs from its author, not only in its way of thinking and feeling, but also in its style of writing; a semi-heteronym only differs from its author in its way of thinking and feeling, not in its style. Thus, in his "Preface to Fictions of the Interlude," Pessoa explains his semi-heteronym Bernardo Soares in this way:

> Bernardo Soares, while differing from me in his ideas, his feelings, and his way of seeing and understanding, expresses himself in the same way I do. He is a different personality, but expressed through my natural style.[17]

Sub-heteronyms, on the other hand, play a fundamentally different role in Pessoa's oeuvre: they are literary personalities entrusted with translating or writing essays about the works of the heteronyms & semi-heteronyms. The labor of Pessoa's sub-heteronyms is to divulge the works of his other literary personalities, and their existence is strictly attached to that labor. But underlying Pessoa's fabrication of all of these other types of heteronyms, are what Pessoa scholars usually call his *pre*-heteronyms. In a famous letter to João Gaspar Simões concerning the genesis of the heteronyms, Pessoa says this:

> Ever since I was a child, it has been my tendency to create around me a fictitious world, to surround myself with friends & acquaintances that never existed.[18]

The first public appearance of a heteronym occurred in the modernist Portuguese review *Orpheu*, in 1915, when Pessoa presented for the first time the "Opiary" and "Triumphal Ode" of Álvaro de Campos. But by that time, he had already conceived and written under the name of several other literary personalities. In his early writings, one finds English and French poetry and prose under the names of literary personalities — preheteronyms —, which constituted a literary laboratory for the creation of his heteronyms. And among the pre-

---

17. Ibid., 313.
18. January 13, 1935. Ibid., 254.

heteronymic documents, one also finds myriad projects for literary works, to be written in different styles, and attributed to different personalities, many of which already have individual biographies. These early projects, assigned to several literary personalities, constitute a pre-heteronymic background for the creation of Pessoa's later heteronyms, and it is during this pre-heteronymic stage that the works of Charles Robert Anon and Alexander Search emerge.

In the Pessoa Archive one finds poems, fiction, and scientific observations attributed to Charles Robert Anon and Alexander Search, and the *Philosophical Essays* are just one part of their production. In the fabrication of these two pre-heteronyms and the texts written in their names, Pessoa begins to develop subjects that clearly influence his later heteronyms and heteronymic works. At the same time, a poetry "animated by philosophy" will be a poetry alive with the highly varied impulse of Pessoa's early philosophical texts. And this is, in effect, what he states in a fragment contemporary to the heteronymic productions, where he discusses the difference between his literary creation and that of the Persian poet Omar Khayyám:

> Omar had one personality; I, fortunately or unfortunately, have none. What I am one hour, I am not the next hour; what I've been one day, the next day I've forgotten. Omar, who is who he is, lives only in one world, which is the external world; I, who am not who I am, live not

only in the external world, but in a successive and diverse internal world. His philosophy, even if he wants to be the same as Omar's, can not at all be the same. Thus, without my consent, I have in me, as if they were souls, the philosophies I criticize; Omar could reject them all, because they were external to him; I can't reject them, because they are myself.

[BNP/E3, 1-2ʳ][19]

Though a pre-heteronym, Pessoa already left this short biographical sketch for (& from) Charles Robert Anon:

> I, Charles Robert Anon,
> being, animal, mammal, tetrapod,
> primate, placental, ape, catar-
> rhyna, □   man;
> eighteen years of age, not
> married (except at odd
> moments) megalomaniac,
> with touches of dipsomania,
> dégénéré superior, poet, with
> pretensions to written humour, citizen
> of the world, idealistic philo-
> sopher, etc. etc. (to spare
> the reader further pains).
>
> In the name of TRUTH,
> SCIENCE and PHILOSOPHIA,

---

19. Originally in Portuguese.

not with bell, book +
candle, but with pen,
ink and paper,
Pass sentence of excom-
munication on all priests and
all sectarians of all
religions in the world.

> *Excomunicabo vos.*
> *Be damn'd to you all.*
> *Ansi-soit-il.*
> *Reason, Truth, Virtue*
> *per C. R. A.*

[BNP/E3, 144C², 5ᵛ a 6ʳ]

This auto-psychography of Charles Robert Anon, at the age of eighteen, succinctly expresses the relation between Pessoa's construction of a pre-heteronym and his new interest in philosophy. In this text, Anon is characterized as an "idealistic philosopher" who fights with pen and ink "in the name of TRUTH, SCIENCE, and PHILOSOPHIA." And, in an English notebook titled "The Transformation Book or Book of Task" [BNP/E3, 48C-1-5], Pessoa left us the following biographical sketch and characterization of Alexander Search, to whom various titles are attributed:

Alexander Search.

Born June 13th 1888, at Lisbon.
Task: all not the province of the other three.

———

1. "The Portuguese Regicide and the Political Situation in Portugal."

2. "The Philosophy of Rationalism."

3. "The Mental Disorder(s) of Jesus."

4. "Delirium."

5. "Agony."

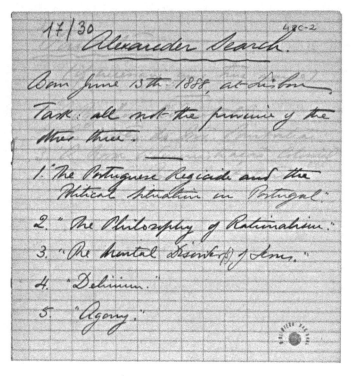

[BNP/E3, 48C-3ʳ]

"The Philosophy of Rationalism," here attributed to Search, is probably a variant title for the "Essay on the Nature and Meaning of Rationalism" presented in this edition — though one cannot be entirely sure. The former title indicates the philosophical concerns of a specific pre-heteronym, side by side with his interest in politics, the problem of madness (or, rather precisely, the madness of Jesus), and poetics.

Pessoa gives Anon's and Search's signatures to some of the texts collected here, whereas others are not explicitly attributed to any personality, and should therefore read as if they were written "anonymously" (all such texts have been designated herein as "unsigned"). This is the case with the essays "On the Nature and Meaning of Rationalism," "On the Idea of Responsibility," "On Error," "On Sensation," "Essay on Heraclitus," "On Thomas Aquinas," and "Essay on Pascal," all of whose authorship can only be attributed with skeptical reserve.[20] In the Pessoa Archive, there are also two extensive reading notebooks from 1906: one signed by Charles Robert Anon, the other by Alexander Search. In Anon's notebook [BNP/E3-13A, 2 et seq.] one finds

---

20. For example, according to some notes about sensation contained in a notebook signed by Anon, we could attribute the "Essay on Sensation" to him. Similarly with the essay "On the Idea of Responsibility," which was originally conceived as a theme to be considered in the project of the "Essay on Free Will," explicitly attributed to Anon (such as the essay "On the Limits of Science," also signed by Anon). In a loose sheet, where Pessoa notes and translates a Greek sentence of Heraclitus [BNP/E3, 133-8], one also finds the signature of Alexander Search. This could demonstrate that the interest in Heraclitus be associated with Search, but it is not sufficient evidence for definitively attributing the material to him. Thus any attribution of the unsigned texts to a specific personality can only be made, according to the clues left by Pessoa, strictly conjecturally. Concerning the "Essay on the Nature and Meaning of Rationalism," we've already noted that it could be interpreted as a variant title of Search's "The Philosophy of Rationalism."

a lengthy list of books, among which are included the names of philosophical figures followed by the titles of their works — Aristotle, Malebranche, Spinoza, Leibniz, Berkeley, Schopenhauer, Hegel, and so on.[21] The same titles are listed in the philosophical reading notebook attributed to Search [BNP/E3, 144H], which orders philosophers' works from "A" to "Z" (see image below: cover).

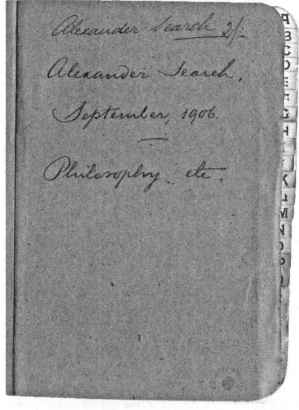

[BNP/E3, 144H]

But as this overlap indicates: while some of Pessoa's *Philosophical Essays* are unattributed, there are also cases where a single text is given different attributions in different contexts.[22] This is the case, for example, with the "Essay on the Idea of Cause," whose fragments are signed both by Search [BNP/E3-15⁴, 99-100] and Anon [BNP/E3, 13A-5aʳ].

Nevertheless, what is reasonably clear is that Pessoa developed his *Philosophical Essays* under the names of several literary personalities, and within the counterpoise or contradictions of several perspectives. As a result, if one expects to find anything like a unitary system in Pessoa's philosophical texts, the going will be rough. In fact, he addresses the virtual impossibility of such unity in the following fragment:

> [...] about a single thing ten thousand thoughts, and ten thousand inter-associations of those ten thousand

---

21. In the notebook designated to Charles Robert Anon, there is a sequence of sheets [BNP/E3, 41-58] stamped with the name of this pre-heteronym, with reference to the readings made by Pessoa in the National Library of Portugal during 1906. In these sheets one finds, just as well, references to Pessoa's philosophical projects. That Search's signature is on the verso of one of these sheets could possibly prove the connection between the two personalities [BNP/E3, 13A-56].

22. This is the case not only with some of the philosophical writings, but also with other texts in the Pessoa Archive, such as poetry and fiction, for there are many cases of multiple attribution of a text to several personalities.

> thoughts arise, and I have no will to eliminate or to arrest these, nor to gather them into one central thought, where their unimportant but associated details might be lost. They pass in me; they are not my thoughts, but thoughts that pass in me.[23]

This passage, probably written in 1907, yields a crucial insight into the writings in question: they represent a stage of experimentation in which Pessoa develops a multiplicity of perspectives to correspond to multiple ways of facing a philosophical problem or "a single thing." These early writings — some pre-heteronymic, some unattributed — adopt different philosophical principles in order to produce different conclusions. To try to reduce these texts to a central unifying thought devoid of contradictions would be to betray Pessoa's chosen way of writing philosophy — when he writes philosophy, he writes *philosophies*.

From the outset, Pessoa gives voice to a plurality of philosophies through a dialogue with Schopenhauer's *Essay on Free-Will*, Pascal's *Pensées*, Kant's *Critique of Pure Reason*, and so on. His reading notebooks and diaries give an account of the various readings that coordinate his philosophical writings. A striking example of this is provided by Schopenhauer's *Essay on Free-Will*. Pessoa owned a French translation of the book and his copy

---

23. Fernando Pessoa, *Escritos Autobiográficos, Automáticos e de Reflexão Pessoal*, 100–101.

shows signs of reading (underlining, comments, &c.).[24]
This book influenced the construction of the elements
for his "Essay on Free-Will," as well as his "Essay on the
Idea of Cause," both of which draw upon and question
the concepts developed in Schopenhauer's work. And
by 1906, Pessoa had also read Kant's *Critique of Pure
Reason* in a French translation by Jules Barni.[25] In Anon's
reading notebook, we find the following statement:

> Friday, 20th April, 1906
>
> Holidays yet. Bibliotheca Nacional; began reading
> *Critique of Pure Reason*, in the French translation by
> Barni.[26]

[BNP/E3, 13A–50ʳ]

Pessoa's reading of the first *Critique* would influence the discussion and definition of rationalism in his "Essay on the Nature and Meaning of Rationalism," a text that has no explicit attribution. There are also examples of minor philosophical works, such as Alfred Fouilée's *La Liberté et le déterminisme*,[27] which served Pessoa as a basis for other essays.

Although Pessoa would later write philosophical texts in Portuguese — and to a lesser extent, in French — it is his English *Philosophical Essays* that are contemporary with his keenest interest in philosophy, and hence that form a backdrop for all of his other philosophical writings and considerations. This edition has been designed to clarify the reach of Pessoa's philosophical writings, and at the same time — in offering a reconstruction of his English essays — to contribute to a more complete knowledge of his substantial philosophical production.

---

24. Cf. Arthur Schopenhauer, *Essai sur le libre arbitre*, tr. by Salomon Reinach (Paris: Félix Alcan, 1903). The reading date of the book, which is kept in Pessoa's Private Library [CFP, 1-135], is listed as "April, 1906."
25. Immanuel Kant, *Critique de Raison Pure, tome I et II*, tr. by Jules Barni (Paris: Germer-Baillière, 1869).
26. Pessoa's copy of this book is not in his Private Library.
27. Alfred Fouillée, *La Liberté et le déterminisme* (Paris: Félix Alcan, 1884).

4

THE ORGANIZATION OF THE PRESENT EDITION & THE *PHILOSOPHICAL ESSAYS*

The present edition is divided in two parts. The first contains the *Philosophical Essays*, reconstructed according to various indications left by Pessoa, while in the second, I present a number of preliminary sketches and other texts that shed light on the essays in Part I.

The first essay in Part I is the unsigned "Essay on the Nature and Meaning of Rationalism." In Pessoa's reading lists & notebooks, or those of his different heteronyms, one finds several indications of his interest in rationalism. For example, in Anon's reading notebook [BNP/E3,13A], one finds references to Thomas Paine's *The Age of Reason* [BNP/E3,13A-8^r], Thomas Child's *Root Principles in Rational and Spiritual Things* [BNP/E3,13A-9^r], and John Mackinnon Robertson's *Letter on Reasoning* [BNP/E3,13A-9^r]. These references are also listed in Search's philosophical reading notebook, while other suggestive titles are cited elsewhere in the Pessoa Archive, such as J.M. Robertson's *Rationalism* [BNP/E3,144D^2-86^r], and Alfred William Benn's *History of English Rationalism in the Nineteenth Century* [BNP/E3,48-50^r]. Nevertheless, that Kant's *Critique of Pure Reason* is central to Pessoa's own notion of rationalism, is evident for instance in this excerpt from the essay on rationalism:

> Kant's great distinction between pure and practical reason ... He was the greatest rationalist the world has ever had thinking upon it. He worked out his own salvation of all reason in that quiet Königsberg, alone with moral law and the stars. He had that little Königsberg where to stand and thence he could move the earth.
>
> [BNP/E3-15²-66ʳ]

This passage reveals the importance of one of Kant's critical distinctions — the difference between pure and practical reason — and how Pessoa uses it to construct his own notion of rationalism. Indeed, Pessoa's rationalistic affirmation that the "only things that can be affirmed as facts are those which reduce experience by reason to the coordination called science" [BNP/E3-15²-62ʳ], is shaped out of Kant's notion of phenomena. All these clues reveal the crucial position of Kant for Pessoa's definition of rationalism.

My reconstruction of the unsigned "Essay on the Nature and Meaning of Rationalism" involves several stages:

1) a first stage corresponds to two manuscript documents, the first entitled "Essay on the Nature and Meaning of Rationalism" [BNP/E3, 15⁵-79], the second simply "*Rationalism*" [BNP/E3, 15⁵-78], which preserve the initial sketches for this essay as a whole. These documents are presented in Part II, section 1.1 as "1ˢᵗ Stage";

2) a second stage relies on two series of manuscript documents titled "Rationalism" [BNP/E3, 15³ – 37 a 45, 133F – 64 a 64a], which serves as an abbreviation of "Essay on the Nature and Meaning of Rationalism." These documents are also transcribed in Part II, section 1.1 as "2ⁿᵈ Stage"; while

3) the third stage moves to a series of nine typewritten documents [BNP/E3, 152 – 62 a 70] that contain Pessoa's final version of the "Essay on the Nature and Meaning of Rationalism," and result from the reconstructive work outlined in the first and second stages. I have added to this sequence of nine typewritten documents a loose text (also typewritten) that opens with the words, "There are two rationalisms" [55G – 24ʳ], plus three other untitled manuscript texts [BNP/E3 – 15¹ – 45ʳ, 46ʳ and 47ʳ], and finally a text entitled "Liberal Rationalism" [15⁵ – 19]. I consider these to belong with the series of nine typewritten documents since they deal with problems that follow in the sequence of these documents. Together, these texts are transcribed as Part I, essay I of this edition. Additionally: in Part II, section 1.2, the unsigned "An Examination of Rationalism" again discusses the role of reason in the constitution of knowledge, but is an autonomous text.

The second essay in Part I is Charles Robert Anon's "Essay on Free-Will." As previously noted, it derives from a reading of Schopenhauer's *Essay on Free-Will* and Fouilée's *La Liberté et le déterminisme*. The development of Anon's "Essay on Free-Will" has a very complex structure that can be also divided into several stages. His interest in free-will is related to his work on the problem of the death penalty. In Anon's reading diary one finds the following excerpt from April 12, 1906:

> Planned and wrote a little of an English work against the death penalty, and, perhaps, against unkind incarceration. Must read books on free-will to be able to attack the death penalty.[28]

Thus, starting with Anon's interest in the question of the death penalty, the development of his interest in the problem of free-will had three main stages:

1) the elaboration of a text called "Against the Death-Penalty" [BNP/E3, 55E-2 e 3] that deals with the question of free-will in the context of Pessoa's defense of the abolition of the death penalty. This unsigned text is presented in Part II, section 2.1;

2) the development of Pessoa's interest in free-will corresponds to the elaboration of an unsigned document titled "Essay on Liberty. Or on [the] Basis of Ethics" [BNP/E3, 48H-61ʳ]. The projects for this essay and the fragments that can be related to it are presented in Part II, section 2.2;

---

28. Fernando Pessoa, *Escritos Autobiográficos, Automáticos e de Reflexão Pessoal*, 34 & 35.

3) the projects and fragments for Anon's "Essay on Free-Will" correspond to Part I, essay 2.

This "Essay on Free Will," which presents the last development of Pessoa's interest in free-will in the early Lisbon notebooks, corresponds to the attempt to demonstrate through his analysis and, in many cases, appropriation of Schopenhauer's and Fouillée's arguments, that our consciousness of free-will is an illusion based on an attribution to the world of our notion of physical liberty. This is precisely what one reads in the following fragment of the "Essay on Free-Will":

> The idea of free-will, in my opinion, has its rise in the application to the moral world of the primitive and natural idea of physical liberty. This application, this analogy is unconscious; and it is also false. It is, I repeat, one of those unconscious errors which we make, one of those false reasoning which we so often and so naturally indulge.
>
> [BNP/E3-23-49ʳ]

The third essay (unsigned) in Part I is "On the Idea of Responsibility." The concept and problems of responsibility were initially conceived by Pessoa as topics to be included in the "Essay on Free-Will." Part of that includes "On Responsibility," a chapter to be developed during the analysis of free-will — as is evident, for example, in the fifth topic of the following project:

INTRODUCTION

On Free-Will

Preface

1. Definitions.
2. History of the Problem.
3. Arguments pro and contra.
4. New Arguments.
5. On Responsibility.
6. Consequences of the inexistence of Free-Will.
7. Conclusion. Character.
8. Index of Chapters and of Contents.

[Apud *Fernando Pessoa, El Eterno Viajero* – 28.8] [29]

---

29. The title *Fernando Pessoa, El Eterno Viajero* (Lisbon: Secretaria de Estado da Cultura, 1981), corresponds to a catalogue compiled by Teresa Rita Lopes and Maria Fernanda Abreu. It contains a selection of facsimiles of Pessoa's writings, including the facsimile of the project transcribed above for the essay "On Free-Will" (identified in the catalogue as "28.8," the number we indicate to identify the document). We weren't able to identify the document correspondent to that facsimile in the Pessoa Archive, so we've transcribed the project directly from that catalogue. In fact, *Fernando Pessoa, El Eterno Viajero* was published in 1981, therefore, five years before the cataloguing of the Pessoa Archive in 1986. During that process, some of the documents were lost, while others are still in the possession of Pessoa's family and, therefore, not catalogued in the Pessoa Archive. We believe that this might be the case with this document.

Nevertheless, in view of the number of writings concerned with the question of responsibility and the basic relevance of this notion, Pessoa's consideration of responsibility would become the subject of an independent essay, "On the Idea of Responsibility."[30] In it, responsibility is anterior to, and more fundamental than, free-will. Thus, in a fragment of this work one reads: "Responsibility is an illusion anterior to that of free-will" [BNP/E3, 15⁴–69ʳ]. Again, the primary character of this illusion is expressed in the following fragment:

> Idea of liberty a purely metaphysical idea.
>
> The primary idea is the idea of responsibility, which is only the application of the idea of cause, by the reference of an effect to its Cause. "That man hits me; I hit him in defence." "That man struck that other man and killed him. I saw him. That man is the cause of the other's death." All this is perfectly true.
>
> Thus we see that the idea of free-will is not a primitive idea at all; that responsibility, founded on a legitimate yet ignorant application of the principle of causality, is the really primitive idea.
>
> In the beginning man is not conscious of any but physical liberty. In the beginning there is no such metaphysical state of mind. The idea of liberty is come by reason, is metaphysical & therefore susceptible of error.
>
> [BNP/E3-23-49ᵛ]

---

30. In fact, "On Responsibility" appears in only one of the three documents concerning the projects for the "Essay on Free-Will." From the chapter "On Responsibility" Pessoa developed the essay "On the Idea of Responsibility."

The fourth essay in Part I is Alexander Search's "Essay on the Idea of Cause," which takes its departure from Schopenhauer's distinction between the several notions of cause in the *Essay on Free-Will*. Let us consider this passage:

> Schopenhauer has divided the idea of Cause into 3 other ideas properly speaking: Causation, excitation and motivation.
>
> [BNP/E3-15⁴-100ʳ]

Here, Search announces the purpose of his essay: to debate and analyze Schopenhauer's idea of cause. And in fact, in the French translation of Schopenhauer's text one reads:

> The principle of causality which rules all the modifications in beings, presents itself under three aspects, corresponding to the triple division of the bodies in inorganic bodies, in plants, and in animals; that is: 1st The Causation, in the strictest sense of the word; 2nd the Excitation (*Reiz*); 3rd finally, the Motivation. It is clear that, under these three different forms, the principle of causality maintains its *a priori* value and that the necessity of the causal nexus subsist in all its strictness.[31]
>
> [CFP/I-135: p.56]

---

31. Le principe de causalité, qui régit toutes les modifications des êtres, se présent sous trois aspects, correspondants à la triple division des corps en corps inorganiques, en plantes, et en animaux; à savoir: 1° La Causation, dans le sens le plus étroit du mot; 2° l'Excitation (*Reiz*); 3° enfin la Motivation. Il est bien

Both of the documents in Part II, section 3 — both of which are attributed to Charles Robert Anon, rather than Search — testify to an interest in Schopenhauer's notion of causality.

The fifth essay (unsigned) in Part I, "On Error," derives from Pessoa's reading of the Platonic dialogue *Theaetetus*. In a fragment for "On Error," one reads the following parenthetical indication: "On Error. A commentary on the *Theaetetus* of Plato" [BNP/E3, 25 - 88ᵛ], while in Anon's reading diary the exact date of his reading is indicated: "November 16th: Plato: *Theaetetus*."[32] The fragments left by Pessoa for this essay discuss the role of sensation in knowledge and lead to his consideration of the *Theaetetus*' argument over whether "Error is in sensation and only in sensation" [BNP/E3, 25 - 88ʳ]. In Part II, section 4, I also present unsigned texts concerning the discussion of error, titled "Fragments with References to the Concept of Sensation."

The sixth essay (unsigned) in Part I is "On Sensation," and this again reflects some of Pessoa's early philosophical readings. Here, one of his most important readings is likely Fouillée's *La Philosophie de Platon*. In a chapter of Fouillée's book, one reads this:

---

entendu que sous ces trois fromes différentes, le principe de causalité conserve sa valeur *à priori*, et que la nécessité de la liaison causale subsiste dans toute sa rigueur.

32. Fernando Pessoa, *Escritos Autobiográficos, Automáticos e de Reflexão Pessoal*, 52.

I. The Sensation

Before the sensation, the intellect remained as if it were asleep, containing in itself the truth, but without knowing it and without experiencing the desire of bringing it to light. Through the sensation the exterior world acts upon it, provokes it, delights it or torments it, finally finishes with its torpor and with its sleep. It sees, it understands, it feels, it knows. <u>Suppress the sensation, you will suppress the knowledge.</u> [33]

[CFP/1-49: p.14]

This passage, which Pessoa underlined, gives some evidence of his interest in sensation, while another book that influenced his considerations concerning sensation is Alfred Binet's *L'Ame et le Corps*. In Binet's text, one finds two chapters on sensation: "De l'objet extérieur nous ne connaissons que des sensations" (bk. I, ch. II); and "La définition de la sensation" (bk. II, ch. II). In Part II, section 4, I collect other texts of Pessoa's that address sensation, among which is a polemical composition: "On Binet's Proof of the World's Existence."[34]

---

33. I. La sensation.

Avant la sensation, l'intelligence était comme endormie, renfermant en elle-même la vérité, mais sans le savoir et sans éprouver le besoin de la mettre au jour. Par la sensation le monde extérieur agit sur elle, la provoque, la réjouit ou la tourmente, la tire enfin de sa torpeur et de son sommeil. Elle voit, elle entende, elle sent, elle connaît. <u>Supprimez la sensation, vous supprimez la connaissance.</u>

The "Essay on Heraclitus," the seventh essay (unsigned) in Part I, contains fragments written by Pessoa in response to his reading of manuals on the history of philosophy. In Anon's reading diary, one also finds many references to the pre-Socratic philosophers as treated in Alfred Weber's *History of Philosophy*, which was probably the main source for Pessoa's knowledge of Heraclitus. The problematic concerning movement, present in the "Essay on Heraclitus," might also be related to Fouillée's *La Philosophie de Platon*, which contains references to Plato's analysis of the Heraclitean problem of becoming.

Part I, essay VIII (unsigned) is transcribed as "On Thomas Aquinas." Pessoa's interest in medieval philosophy is suggested by the following note from Anon's reading diary:

> May 13th (Sunday)
>
> A dark and rainy day; remained at home. Read about Scholastic Philosophy in Vallet.[35]

---

34. For further material on sensation, see: Nuno Ribeiro, "The Plural Writing & the Sensationist Movement," *Hyperion: On the Future of Aesthetics*, Vol. V, Nº 2 (November 2010) 73–95. Aside from a brief essay on sensationism, this publication contains selections and translations from Pessoa's sensationist writings.
35. Fernando Pessoa, *Escritos Autobiográficos, Automáticos e de Reflexão Pessoal*, 38 and 39.

The book Pessoa refers to here is Pierre Vallet's *Histoire de la Philosophie*, where one finds a section entitled, " Art. II — Seconde période de la philosophie scolastique: son apogée; XIIIe siècle," which is partially devoted to the study of Aquinas. This appears to have been the source of Pessoa's acquaintance with his philosophy, while Pessoa's questions in "On Thomas Aquinas" are a consequence of Vallet's treatment of thirteenth-century philosophy. This essay also deals with the problem and critique of the reconciliation between God's physical pre-motion and freedom of the will, which is referred to in Vallet's book.

The brief fragments of the unsigned "Essay on Pascal" — Part I, essay IX — express his interest in and reading of Pascal. In Pessoa's Private Library, one finds Pascal's *Pensées* [CFP, 1-116] and *Les Provinciales* [CFP, 1-117], both of which contain underlinings by Pessoa. Nevertheless, his reading of Pascal was critical, and this essay constitutes a critique of the influence of the Catholic Church on thought. The arguments used are similar to some of Nietzsche's, and Pessoa's interest in Nietzsche is substantiated by his reading lists. For instance, in Search's 1906 reading notebook, we find entries for Fouillée's *Nietzsche et l'immoralisme* and Lichtenberger's *Philosophie de Nietzsche*, while it is well

---

36. In the book *Fernando Pessoa e Nietzsche: O pensamento da pluralidade*, we present the clues of Pessoa's reading of Nietzsche, based on philological evidence contained in the Pessoa Archive.

established that Pessoa read Nietzsche directly and in secondary sources from 1906 onwards.[36] It is likely Nietzsche, then, who inspired Pessoa's critical evaluation of Pascal.

The tenth & last essay in Part I is "On the Limits of Science." It is signed by Anon and is one of the briefest philosophical texts 'Pessoa' wrote; it deals with the problem of empirical illusion and the immortality of the soul. The title indicates Anon's interest in science, which is amply attested to in his other readings and writings. A single example of this, from his Private Library, is G. H. Lewes' book *Science and Speculation*, which contains underlinings and marginal notes in Pessoa's hand.

5

CRITERIA OF PUBLICATION AND PROVENANCE OF THE TEXTS

This edition presents a transcription and organization of Fernando Pessoa's *Philosophical Essays*, all of which were written in English and are held at the Fernando Pessoa Archive in the Biblioteca Nacional de Portugal (BNP). There is one exception, a document correspondent to one of the projects for the essay "Free-Will," a reference I wasn't able to identify in the Pessoa Archive and which was therefore transcribed from the facsimile contained in the catalogue *Fernando Pessoa, El Eterno Viajero*. I am entirely responsible for editing and structuring the texts, but have organized them — as far as was possible — according to clues in Pessoa's relevant outlines. Other indications have been gleaned from original manuscripts and typescripts of Pessoa's, although philosophical materials are often catalogued inconsistently in the Pessoa Archive.

In transcribing the material, I have always kept the first version of a word or sentence wherever there is more than one variant. I have adopted this criterion since Pessoa left, in many cases, more than one variant for a word or sentence without indicating his preference, for he never made a final and complete version of these texts. Pessoa used to write a first word or sentence and then insert variants that he could include in place of the first; but considering the optional and open character of these variants, I have taken his first version as a criterion. Regarding "free will," the phrase is sometimes in lower case, capitalized, hyphenated, etc. — all such variations are Pessoa's and have been strictly followed. Finally, any textual variants, as well as genetic notes, are given in footnotes that also contain any elements that were struck out, and any other changes made in the original text. This will enable general readers to get a sense of the compositional process of these texts, and provide Pessoa scholars with a valuable critical apparatus. For the transcription of these texts, the following symbols have been used:[37]

~~xxxxxx~~ struck-out segment

x x x x x x ↑xxxxxx segment inserted above

x x x x x x ↓xxxxxx segment inserted below

x x x x x x →xxxxxx segment inserted on the right side

x x x x x x ←xxxxxx segment inserted on the left side

x x x x x x /xxxxxx\ variant segment

XXXXXX underlined segment

| x x x x | segment doubted by the author

† illegible word

☐ empty space left by the author

[x|y] substitution by superposition, in the relation [~~substituted~~ | substitute]

|* x x x x | conjectural reading

[x x x x] segment added by the editor

[…] absence of material support [damaged segment in the original material]

---

37. Some of the symbols used for the transcription of the texts present in this edition can be found in the following bibliographical reference: Nuno Venturinha, *Lógica, Ética e Gramática — Wittgenstein e o Método da Filosofia* (Lisbon: Imprensa Nacional-Casa da Moeda, 2010). Others were adapted or created for the purpose and specificity of a general edition of Pessoa's writings — these symbols will be used in future editions of Pessoa's fragments.

PART I.
Philosophical Essays

1 – Essay on the Nature and Meaning of Rationalism

[15² – 62 – 70]

Rationalism

Rationalism holds that the only things that can be affirmed as facts are those[1] which reduce experience by reason to the coordination called science.[2] Rationalism holds that all things outside this are simply unknown,[3] or as yet unknown; but it does not affirm either that they are unknowable or still less that they are false. For what cannot be proved cannot also be disproved. The affirmation that Christ is God, for example, cannot be rejected by a Rationalist because it cannot be affirmed by him. It may be an error; it may be the vision of a higher sight — the Rationalist cannot determine which it is, because he does not know a thing to be wrong unless he can subject it to reason, and he cannot affirm a sense to be non-existent simply because he himself has not got it.

For this reason atheism is not rationalism at all, and no atheist can describe himself as a rationalist unless he

---

1. tho[e|s]e
2. to ↑ ^{the coordination called} science
3. ~~as yet~~ unknown

ON THE NATURE & MEANING OF RATIONALISM

ignores[4] the meaning of rationalism, of atheism, or of both. The truth is that atheism is not a form[5] of disbelief, but of belief. It is commonly supposed that an atheist is a man who does not believe in the existence of God. This is wrong, for he is not so negative. He is a man who believes in the existence of not-God. Hence his positiveness, his happiness, and that[6] buoyant faith of a militant unchristian.

Rationalism is knowledge bounded by ignorance.[7] It is no more than this. Where atheism is intolerant or contemptuously tolerant, rationalism is fully tolerant. The pity is that it is not an attitude that can be popular, and this is one of the reasons why real rationalists are seldom, if ever democratic.[8] It is also one of the reasons why they are so ready to deal kindly with what the staunch atheist would regard as gross and immoral superstition. Where they do not know, they ignore.[9] The atheist knows that palmistry is wrong. If he has not tested it, or cannot test it,[10] the rationalist says nothing.

Neither can it be said that rationalism[11] and agnosticism are the same thing. Agnosticism directly implies

---

4. i[i|g]nores
5. f[ł|o]rm
6. ↓and th[e|a]t
7. knowledge /↑science\ bounded by ignorance /↑agnosticism\
8. ~~very~~ seldom, ↑if ever democratic
9. superstition. ← Where they do not know, they ignore.
10. test~~ed~~ it
11. ~~agn~~ rationalism

the[12] affirmation that the unknown is unknowable. Rationalism cannot say of the unknown that it is so far known as to be known to be unknowable. A wider[13] agnosticism may affirm that even the known is unknowable — a far more tenable and rational proposition. In this case it[14] may be called Absolute Rationalism — the belief that nothing can be believed unless it is brought[15] under reason, with the addition of the belief that nothing can be brought under reason.

[63ʳ]

Some agnostics distinguish between the unknown of science and the unknown of metaphysics — the lesser and the greater unknowns, Ursa Minor and Ursa Major[16] of an inexistent sky.

Scepticism may also be confounded with rationalism. But the sceptic, if he really be one, has no belief at all; the rationalist does believe in reason. To a certain extent, as far as reason, the rationalist is a believer. As a matter of fact, he is wholly a believer. It is because the sceptic is not a believer that he destroys himself: scepticism, as in Pascal, was ever the fore-prey of mysticism.

---

12. th[a|e]
13. wider /↑ sadder\
14. ↑ [w|H]ere agnosticism In this case it
15. b[ө|r]ought
16. Ma[ʜ|j]or

ON THE NATURE & MEANING OF RATIONALISM

The half-sceptic speaks like Socrates, I know only that I know nothing. The whole sceptic speaks like Francisco Sanches:[17] *Haud scio me nihil scire*, I do not even know if I know nothing.

(My countryman is said to have preceded Descartes, probably because he came before him. But that is mere chronology. I do not believe he influenced Descartes (vide/Stark).[18] Metaphysical speculation is not one of the violent pastimes of the Portuguese; even Spinoza had to be also a Jew and a Dutchman to find a private universe. The most any Portuguese ancestor of his could have done was to help to find the present earth at the[19] opposite end.)

☐ the transcendental atheism of the Buddhists.

Modern scientific speculation has brought the old atheists to their lack of senses and has given them a finite world, robbing them of the now unfashionable infinity, which they had taken from God to give it to the blackness of mute space and the emptiness of dull time.

☐ that negative omnipresent God of the Indian mystics who rises down to himself through the black Jacob's ladder of an increasingly[20] depersonalized autolatry.

---

17. Francisco Sanches (1550–1622) was a Portuguese philosopher. He wrote a book entitled *Quod nihil Scitur* (*That nothing is known*), which is said to have influenced Descartes' method of doubt.
18. Descartes → (vide/Stark)
19. the ↓ some
20. a ↓ an increasingly

[64ʳ]
Rationalism

For[21] human experience includes very little that is rational. That is the primary fact the rationalists must undergo.

□ the terrible intellectual phenomenon of these |*being| such a thing is vain, which is a part of the just spiritual phenomenon of these being anything at all.[22]

Those strange aesthetes of the lesser mind, who can understand the paradoxical beauty of a genius clothed among fools with obscurity,[23] but not the paradoxical splendour of the God crucified among thieves.[24]

Rationalism gathers in very little, because reason has exact[ly] very little scope in[25] which to operate. When we leave the figures which denote the coefficient of expansion of iron, we have only the mystery of iron left over.

The strength of rationalism is in its narrowness for all strength is a narrowness.[26] It leaves us ever humble[27] before the infinite remainder.

It may be thought that this is why great Christians, like St. Thomas Aquinas, were rationalists. But the point

---

21. |For|
22. ↑ the terrible ~~phen~~ intellectual phenomenon of these being such a thing is vain, which is a part of the just ~~higher~~ spiritual phenomenon of these being anything at all.
23. clothed ^/↑ celled\ ← among fools with ^/↑ in\ obscurity,
24. ↓ ᵃ God crucified among ~~the~~ thieves.
25. has ← exact very little scope [o|i]n
26. for all strength is a narrow↑ness.
27. ↓ ever humble

is the other way. St. Thomas was neither a Christian nor a rationalist. He was only a Catholic and a reasoner. The rationalist inverts the position which he put. He made, as the old phrase has it, philosophy the handmaid of theology. But the rationalist, who has no use for theology, which is the affectation of mysticism, considers philosophy as no more than[28] the poetry of thinking.

All I want to give is an expression to a new mood in the withdrawal from speculating.

The materialist is sure. The rationalist is aware.

☐ and man who would not forget to † a knight with "God"? Is not St. Paul worth the Saint; for this is[29] no etiquette ☐

[65ʳ]
Rationalism

If this slight book be read by any rationalist who had Paine for governess, he will, when this point is reached, have pleasure in finding me out. But, like Mr. Jingle, I would rather have that than that he found me in.

For this is only a notion of reality. Reality is not only stones and plants, with a moving sprinkling[30] of animals. It is also the dreams, the visions, the mystical experiences, of the substance and passing of mankind. Christ may

---

28. ~~makes theology~~ ↓ considers philosophy as no more than
29. for ↑ this is
30. a ↑ moving sprinkling

not be real as reality, but has been real as an ideality. For the realist, who is the rationalist, that is as enough as the stars. The ideal men have loved is as real as the woman men have loved, for the love is the one actual thing.

The end of reason is a weariness of thinking. Yet reason is so strong that even its weariness is a part of its strength and we dream rationally if we have learnt reason.

....

|The rumour[31] is abroad that the Gods are dead. But the Gods, being immortal, are very lively.|

|We may conceive the total of mankind as the passengers and crew of a ship of fools, left helmless on an uncharted ocean. They will make games last while life endures, and have death for a certainty, with some expectation of being saved, for there may be a better map for a ship coming[32] on their way.|

[66ʳ]
Rationalism

... dreary as a languid gorgeousness, like that of *Faerie Queene*, which not even Edmund Spenser ever dared to read through in all the entirety there is of it.

□ the old bourgeoisie of the wrong rationalism,[33] from

---

31. rumours
32. [w|c]oming
33. of ↑ the wrong rationalism,

poor old Thomas Paine, who ☐ to Mr. J. M. Robertson,[34] who dispossessed[35] God of infinity in favour of that universal interval called space.

It is brilliant to the point of nauseousness...

But the rationalist makes no conflict with any man's opinions. He admits the possibility of the existence of God and the possibility of that God being the wood idol of the African wilds. Like Baudelaire, he would say to the disgusted sailor who wanted to throw that idol into a corner,[36] *"Et si c'était le vrai Dieu?"*

---

34. John Mackinnon Robertson (1856–1933) was a member of the English rationalist movement that emerged in the United Kingdom between the end of the XIX century and the beginning of the XX century. In Pessoa's Private Library, there are twenty-three books by Robertson: *Pioneer Humanists* [CFP, 1-129]; *Pagan Christs* [CFP, 2-54]; *Browning and Tennyson as Teachers* [CFP, 8-475]; *A Short History of Freethought* [CFP, 1-130]; *Christianity and Mythology* [CFP, 2-49]; *Essays on Sociology* [CFP, 3-67]; *Criticisms* [8-476]; *Essays in Ethics* [CFP, 1-128]; *Modern Humanists* [CFP, 3-68]; *A Short History of Christianity* [CFP, 2-55]; *Explorations* [CFP, 2-51]; *The Genuine in Shakespeare* [CFP, 8-472]; *The Baconian Heresy* [CFP, 8-471]; *Charles Bradlaugh* [CFP, 9-61]; *The Dynamics of Religion* [CFP, 2-50]; *The Saxon and Celt* [CFP, 3-69]; *The Problem of "Hamlet"* [CFP, 8-474]; *"Hamlet" Once More* [CFP, 8-473]; *Jesus & Judas* [CFP, 2-53]; *The Evolution of States* [CFP, 3-66]; *The Historical Jesus* [CFP, 2-52]; *William Archer as Rationalist* [CFP, 8-13], a collection of writings edited by Robertson; *The Philosophical Works of Francis Bacon* [CFP, 1-3], edited with an introduction by Robertson.
35. disposses[s]ed
36. Baude[al|la]ire, he would say to the ↑ disgusted sailor who wanted to throw that idol into a corner, in disgust

Religion is an emotional need of mankind. The rationalist may not want it, but he has to admit that other people may. It[37] is emotional but it is also a need.

There are conflicts between the pure and the practical reason. The rationalist admits Catholicism but he cannot admit the application of that intolerance which is the legitimate right of the Catholic within himself. The tolerant man draws the line at the intolerance of others. He preaches peace and must kill in self-defence.

Kant's great distinction between pure and practical reason...... He was the greatest rationalist the world has ever had thinking upon it. He worked out his own salvation of all reason in that quiet Königsberg, alone with moral law and the stars. He had that little Königsberg where to stand and thence he could move the earth.

I pay the tribute of thankfulness to that full and exact learning which has been deprived of its due recognition. But, if I honour Mr. Robertson for the learning which he has, I cannot respect him for the rationalism which he has forgotten to have. He is the irrationalist pure and simple; there[38] is no third of reason in his believing soul. He even believes in the infinity of space and the eternity of time, and I wonder what science or experience has taught him that those incommensurables exist.[39]

---

37. ~~It is an emotional need~~ It
38. ~~thre~~ there
39. wonder what ← science or experience has ↓ ~~confirm~~ / ↓ can have\ taught him that those |* incommensurables| ~~es~~ exist

[67ʳ]
Rationalism

All science is, substantially, an attempt at science.[40] Even if reason itself did not warn us against the conferring of too much truth upon our generalizations, which[41] are necessarily always hasty, and upon our observations,[42] which are necessarily always imperfect, the historical experience of scientific theories would give our conjectures[43] that advice. The history of science and of knowledge has seen, so many truths sink into mere speculations or into provisional dreams,[44] that the historian of our minor, as that of our major, philosophy may put a constant query to the end of any and every paragraph[45] he indict. Even the dearest littlenesses of science may to-morrow be subverted by great cyclones of mind. We may have to abandon the coefficient of expansion of iron. We may have to controvert Boyle's Law. It is not impossible to formulate, in a sort of tired dream, the negation of the choicest principles of our external sureties.[46] Even two and two may

---

40. an attempt ↑ at science /↑ seeing\.
41. ,whei which
42. ↑ upon our observations,
43. speculation ↑ conjectures
44. truth sink like so many truths sink into ↑ mere speculations or ↑ into provisional dreams,
45. ↑ constant query to the end of ↑ any and every paragraph
46. sureties /(assurances)\ /(certainties)\.

one day cease to be four, to a brighter [47] understanding of the surface and femininity of things.

Yet, since we have no better assurance than reason for the objectivity of certainty, to take a thing as true because it can be proved is yet an excusable [48] shift of our unknowing. In common with all men, each of us has [49] no more than the objective universe, which we may test together, [50] & the principles of reason, by which we can communicate without our souls. Truth is unattainable, but logic is intelligible. Ghosts may be things, but things are things, even if they be ghosts. We must keep to the world that has been given us, and to the manner of test that we have been allowed, or, at the least, [51] have not been deprived of. If a God has made us, it is a sort of blasphemy to doubt the world he made us in and with, and the reason which he gave us as the means for the understanding of that world. If deeper things in our souls reveal objective truths deeper than visible things, and if subtler [52] operations of our minds yield more certain results than reason, we have no power to distinguish, having [53] nothing clearer than our senses, or to criticize, having nothing more

---

47. brighter /↑ deeper and ~~fren~~ ↓ stranger\
48. excusab~~b~~le
49. ~~we have~~ ↑ each of us has
50. ~~in common~~ ↑ together
51. ~~at any rate~~ ↑ at the least
52. ↑ objective truths deeper than visible things, and [o|i]f subtler
53. to distingui[g|s]h, hav[e|i]ng

coherent than our logic. Perhaps God[54] makes a mockery of the things he has himself given us, and plays hide-and-seek with his own self. For all we know, this may be possible. But, as wise men, we will take the gift we see and use [the] tools we have received; the rest we shall leave to the action of Fate and to the hidden purpose if these be one of the unknown substance[55] of things.

[68ʳ]
Rationalism

The scientific spirit means three things: (1) the holding as actually (or, at least, provisionally) true only those laws or facts which have been subjected to an objective test, which anyone, given the culture, the instruments and the opportunity, may equally well apply; (2) the holding as actually (or, at least, provisionally) false of the[56] doctrines or pseudo-facts which directly contradict such laws or facts and are either insusceptible not by nature, but by statement,[57] of objective proof or, being susceptible to it, are not or have not been brought to it; (3) the holding as unknown as to their truth those theories or ideas which, being[58] of a nature wholly incommensurable with the

---

54. ← Perhaps God
55. ↓ to the hidden purpose ↓ if these he own of the unknown /↓ verted\ substance
56. } of the
57. insusceptible /↑ irreducible \ not by nature, but by statement,
58. ~~doctrines or~~ theories or ideas which, ~~are either~~ being

laws and facts which can be verified objectively, are, by that very nature, insusceptible of objective proof.

This means, to exemplify, that we can hold by coefficient of expansion of iron as being a certain proportional figure;[59] we will not hold by a mystic theory which,[60] without a counter-proof equally objective, may affirm that the coefficient in point is another one; we will neither hold nor not hold by such mystic doctrine independent of that application. The proof that the literal interpretation of the statements of Genesis as to the creation of the world is wrong does not affect the metaphysical principles of the religions based on that Genesis. It affects solely the doctrine of physical creation, in so far as it is thus understood.

When a man of "science" says that, as a man of science, he does not[61] accept the doctrine of the Trinity, he is talking like anything except a man of science. All that he can say, as a man of science, is that he not only has not, but cannot have, any opinion on the doctrine of the trinity. He may also say, as a man — not of science but of mankind —, that he does not believe in the doctrine of the Trinity; in the same capacity, he may say that he does believe in it. He is entitled to either affirmation of faith; but, be it negative or positive, it is always an affirmation of faith. The moment he makes it he has ceased

---

59. figure proportional to the length of the proportional figure;
60. wheih which,
61. sciencie, he disbeliev does not

to be a man of science at all. He has become merely a man.[62]

This seems very simple, but human perverseness seems to make it as difficult as all final simplicities are. If, however, a mystic[63] putting forth that physical doctrine, affirm that it is linked with the essence of his spiritual[64] doctrine and that it is a true type and figurement of it, he should not complain[65] if, his own statement being taken as he has given it, the general[66] theory be held wrong on the score of the particular application[67] being proved wrong.

[69ʳ]
Rationalism

Rationalism. Theoretic Rationalism. Practical Rationalism.

Sociology is simply a baser metaphysics. It is so far metaphysics that it seems to be a substitute for it, metaphysical and sociological speculation being generally in the inverse quantity at the same time.

It is easy to defend law and order[68] as necessary to civilization. But Athens was never orderly & the Italian

---

62. merely a man. ← justly also, which may be more or less, sufficient: he has become just a man
63. mystic /↑ religiousist\
64. affirms that it is linked with the sess essence of his spi[t|r]itual
65. compl[ia|ai]n
66. essential ↑ general
67. the ↓ particular application
68. order and law and order

Republics of the Middle Age and of the Renascence had very little order & very little law; yet if the creation of art and culture which distinguished them be not civilization or one of its distinctive characteristics, then civilization is its own opposite. It is easy to contend that a unified nation is essential to its own life; yet Greece, which created the mind of the civilized world, was never the whole of itself, and Italy was best scattered than united, in so far as results to mankind in general are a valid test. It is easy to defend any sociological theory. As in everything, except the bare useless facts,[69] the theory is worth what the theorist is worth, and all is made up, in the ultimate, of aspects of truth.[70]

The legal profession is an immoral and absurd one, but we all[71] counsel of our beliefs, and the better sophist wins — fortunately only temporarily — the futile case he has put himself into.[72]

Some, like Kant, make their philosophies out of themselves. Others, like Nietzsche, make their philosophies out of the negation of themselves. The placid man is placid in his philosophy. The sick man is the philosopher of strength □

Slavery is perfectly defensible. We cannot defend it because Christian morality excludes slavery, and Chris-

---

69. the theo except the bare useless ↑|↑ cosmic| facts.
70. aspects of untruth. /↓ the possibility of truth\
71. ↑ we were all
72. put ↓ high / ↓higher\ himself into

tian morality is one of the bases of our civilization. The death penalty can be defended, but it will not pass the emotional test. The Inquisition can be defended, and it has been defended. But it will not pass the cultural test — it is rebutted, not by any valid argument, which cannot be emptied of force, but by the rationalistic individualism which the Greeks have given us for the soul of our mind.

[70ʳ]
Rationalism

The Christian ethics may be, as Nietzsche puts it, the ethics of slaves. It is, however, our ethics. We have not to say that we do not want that ethics; we can but say that we are slaves. (We may accept Nietzsche's assertion, but we must accept the ethics. It is possible that that ethics is indeed the ethics of slaves; if it be so, then we are slaves and that is our ethics.)

When any man defends cruelty or lust or treason, he may do so with the full armoury of an intellectual arsenal he was born with for a soul; but he speaks to sticks[73] and stones when he would persuade more of us than the surface of our possible reasons to agree with him. We may be cruel, lustful, or treasonable by our passions;

---

73. *In the original document Pessoa writes "stocks" instead of "sticks," presumably by mistake. We've corrected this word since the original idiom in English is not "stocks and stones" but "sticks and stones."*

we cannot be so by our emotions. The door[74] of those theories is definitely blocked in our civilization: it is blocked by the Cross.

The rationalist does not assert that Greek Culture is the best culture: he asserts that, good or not, it is the culture we have. The rationalist does not assert the Roman Order is the best type of order: he asserts that, for better or for worse,[75] it has been wedded to the substance of ourselves. The rationalist does not assert that Christian Ethics is the best possible ethics: he asserts that it is the only one possible to our emotions. The rationalist does not assert that the internationalist civilization created by the Portuguese discoveries and the |*Greek| democratization[76] of learning is the best type of civilization: he asserts that it is ours. For whether it should be there or not, (he asserts that) it is here. There is no more ease in shaking[77] off Greek Culture, Roman Order, or Christian Ethics than there is in, by the use of some transcendental extension of Mr. Wells' Time-Machine, reversing the film of history and disiscovering[78] & reunpeopling[79] the transoceanic world.

---

74. ~~The shadow of the cross~~ The door
75. ~~best or worst,~~ for better or for worse,
76. ↑|*Greek| democratization /↑ hellenization\
77. ~~shak~~ shaking
78. *As is in the original*: "disiscovering" means here the contrary of "discovering."
79. ~~carrying~~ reversing the film of history and ~~un~~↑dis iscovering and ~~unpeopl~~ reunpeopling

As we cannot repudiate our parents or divorce our ancestors, or divorce our mother to be an ex-mother,[80] we cannot make a secure statement that we owe nothing to the fathers or will henceforward have owed them nothing. We may pay or not our[81] debts, we may right or not have debts — we cannot say they were something which is not particularly done.[82]

[55G – 24ʳ]

There are two rationalisms. There is a lower, or fetishistic, rationalism which is that of rationalists[83] commonly so called, and commonly so calling themselves; and there is a higher rationalism. Both believe — at bottom this is, like the bottom of everything else, an unverifiable[84] belief — that reason is all that we have, or the best we have,[85] to investigate truth. The two differ as to what they consider the truth that can be investigated. The lower rationalism is still captive of the old metaphysical myth — that reason can reach metaphysical conclusions. The higher rationalism, basing on the prem-

---

80. our parents ←or divorce our ancestors, or divorce our ~~father~~ ↑mother to be an ex-~~father~~ ↑mother

81. ↑or not our

82. ↑or not have debts — we cannot say they were something w[hich] is not ↓particularly done.

83. of ~~the~~ rationalists

84. *In the original, Pessoa has "inverifiable." Possible authorial lapse.*

85. we have, ~~and the most that~~ or the best we have

ise that all knowledge comes from the senses, and that reason is not a sense, cannot admit the possibility of reason more than sifting the data of the senses; and as there are no known senses (unless the mystics are right, which we cannot verify to universal satisfaction) which supply metaphysical data, reason is powerless to arrive at any conclusion as to the fundamentals of being. All faiths, however absurd they may seem, or contradictory, are therefore possible; they cannot be denounced as false; they must simply be let live as probabilities that never can be verified. This leads to tolerance without an effort.

The attitude of higher rationalism receives its symbol in that celebrated anecdote, which is related of Baudelaire. A naval officer, a friend of his, who had just returned from a long colonial voyage, was showing him a fetish he had brought back; he showed him with disgust that wooden object, the astonishing idol of a human race. And, as he, after having shown it, was going to throw it in disgust into a corner, Baudelaire laid sudden hands upon his arm. "Stop!" he said, "What if it were the true God?" — *Et si c'était le vrai Dieu?* — This[86] is the higher rationalism, both in essence and in tone.

The two rationalisms split, again, over the sociological problem. It is almost invariable that the lower rationalist should be a democrat, a believer in that myth called "the people." As he is generally an atheist — that is to say, a believer with a minus sign — he caries the typical

---

86. T[j|h]is

attitude of belief into a concrete sphere, as all believers do. Where one believes in the Pentateuch, another believes in Democracy.

[15¹ – 45ʳ]

The monism of Force-matter has become, as you know, old; it has been superseded by the Force-Monism of Gustave Le Bon.[87] The blind, stupid, unscrupulous philosophy (for so it is called) of Haeckel[88] has grown old in[89] its metaphysical aspect.

The lack[90] of criticism of reason, by which your system is dogmatic, is the cause of this. What affirms the right of reason to pursue the infinite? Scientific prejudice,

---

87. Gustave Le Bon (1841-1931) was a psychologist, sociologist, and amateur physicist. His work concerned the psychology of the masses and the evolution of social forces. In the field of physics he developed many theories concerning the evolution of matter. In Pessoa's Private Library, there are three books by Le Bon: *L'évolution de la matière* [CFP, 1-81]; *L'évolution des forces* [CFP, 1-82]; and *La Psychologie politique et la défense sociale* [CFP, 1-83].
88. Ernst Haeckel (1834-1919) was a German naturalist and one of the great figures of positivism. He is known to be one of the most important divulgers of Darwin's works. In Pessoa's Private Library, there are four books, in French translation, by Haeckel: *Les merveilles de la vie* [CFP, 1-65]; *Origine de l'homme* [CFP, 5-17]; *Histoire de la création des êtres organisés d'aprés les lois naturelles* [CFP, 5-16]; *Les énigmes de l'univers* [CFP, 1-64].
89. grown ↑ old in
90. ~~Thus for instance infinity of matter~~ The lack

convention — ultimately in some cases intellectual dishonesty.⁹¹ Common sense is the worst enemy of philosophy.

[15¹ – 46ʳ]

The second reason for differing from your system is the ⁹² numerous inconsequences of scientific thought. Any really profound thinker, rationalist or not, will grasp at the joining of the ideas of matter and of eternity, not to speak of those of eternity and infinity and of evolution. Scientific inquiry and observation blunt the reasoning ⁹³ powers; there is no sure way of training the mind in dialectics than reasoning independent of observation.⁹⁴

Rationalism is dogmatic, and it is not a system of philosophy. Telescopes ⁹⁵ search the sky and, as they find no limit, they declare matter infinite. But such is no scientific method. Such is a pure assumption, which is the outcome of your idea of Rationalism. How do you know that reason has the power to affirm infinite multiplication.

[15¹ – 47ʳ]

The foundations of morals are triple: instinct, which

---

91. cases ↑intellectual dishonesty
92. is that is the
93. blunts ↑the reasoning
94. other sure way of training the mind in reasoning ↑dialectics than reasoning independ[a|ᵗᵉ]nt of observation
95. How Telescopes

produces civics; obedience, which produces inhibition; reason, which produces harmony in action.

Reason, by itself, is not moral, because there is no moral to come out from reason. Reason does not create; it merely limits.

A true rationalist is incapable of altruism, because he cannot see, by reason, any reason for altruism. Morality is irrational. But life itself is irrational, and morality is fundamental as being such.

[15⁵–19]
Liberal Rationalism
1. Chapter on: *Fallacies*

There are two errors that may be committed in this respect. One is to make metaphysics a science, the other to make science a metaphysics. The first any theist commits; the second is committed for instance by[96] Professor Haeckel in his "Riddles of the Universe."

Let us abandon, indeed, metaphysics for science, but, doing so, let us remember that science does not *substitute* metaphysics; its province is another. If a man attempt to fly and fail, we may laugh and abandon the idea of flying, by walking; but we must say that we are flying. It is into this error that many scientists fall, materialists or deists, Sir Andrew Lang[97] or Haeckel or Brüchner.[98]

---

96. committed ↑ for instance by

[19ᵛ]

Christianity, anthropomorphism can be attacked — at least attacked by science. Pure deism never — its form is another. Quite outside (if not above) Science.

---

97. Andrew Lang (1844-1912) was a Scottish poet, novelist, literary critic, and translator. He became known for his collection of fairy tales and folk stories, as well as for his translation (in collaboration with others) of Homer's *Iliad* and *Odyssey*. He also developed work in the field of the psychical sciences, and later became president of the Society for Psychical Research.
98. Ludwig Brüchner was a German physicist and philosopher and is known as a partisan of materialism. In Pessoa's Private Library, there are two works, in French translations, by him: *Force et matière* [CFP, 1-15]; *L'homme selon la science* [CFP, 1-16].

II – Essay on Free-Will

Projects

[15ʳ– 35ʳ]

Essay on Free-Will

Chapters:

The metaphysical arguments.
The social and scientific arguments.
Genesis & explanation of the pseudo-idea of Free-Will.
Responsibility.
Conclusion and summary.
The Psychological arguments.

[15ʳ– 34ʳ]

On Free-Will

1. Definitions.
(2. History of the problem.)
3. Metaphysical.
4. Psychological.
5. Social, *moral, juridical*.
6. Fatalism.
7. Free-Will[99] before Science.
8. Determinism and its arguments.
9. Character.

---

99. F[ree-]W[ill]

[*Apud* Fernando Pessoa, El Eterno Viajero — 28.8]

Charles Robt. Anon.
───────────────
C. R. Anon.

On Free-Will

Preface

Part I
    1. History of the Question.
    2. Arguments pro and contra.
    3. New *Arguments*.

Part II
    4. Responsibility.
    5. Consequences.

On Free-Will

Preface
1. Definitions.
2. History of the Problem.
3. Arguments pro and contra.
4. New Arguments.
5. On Responsibility.
6. Consequences of the inexistence of Free-Will.
7. Conclusion. Character.
8. Index of Chapters and of Contents.

Fragments

[13 – 20ʳ]

The will does not exist. It exists within the sphere of Feeling, for it is the necessary adjunct of that psychological faculty.

Charles Robert Anon[100]

The faculty or faculties of the mind united to an external □ produce the act. Sometimes there is a conflict of faculties,[101] of impulses; the strongest, or the most strongly aided predominates.

[15¹ – 17]
On Free Will

The Will is the Cause
The Body is the Instrument
The Act is the Effect

Important

The dynamists say that our impossibility of defining force proves that we are ourselves *forces*.

---

100. Ch[arles] R[ober]t Anon.
101. faculty ↑ or faculties of the mind united to an external □ produce the act. Sometimes there is a conflict of ~~emo~~ ↑ faculties

Can it not more surely be said that an impossibility to define the idea of Being, which is our first idea, proves us [as] parts of Being?

[15¹ – 30ʳ]

An indeterminate will is an infinity in point of will. Two such wills are equal; how can they produce different [102] effects? Moreover, what is this of an infinite thing cause of a finite thing?

The perpetual movement of the Universe is the act of the Power behind it. Aristotle's Pure Act.

The Unknown { Being   Not-Being
               Power   Act

[15¹ – 31]

How[103] do unnatural things result from nature? How is it that there are cripples etc.? By some infringement of the laws of nature. But these cripples, since they exist, are also natural. How did man infringe the Laws of nature? Was it by free-will? Was it by inclination?

The animal is all inclin-[31ᵛ]ation and he is *generally* according to nature.

What then is there in man contrary to this?

---

102. diff[eren]t
103. ~~Of the Necessity~~
     ~~How many times do we~~
     How

But also, since man is the descendant of the animal, man can have but inclinations. What he can have new is other inclinations, which are of nature opposed to those which he holds in common with the animal. What is the explanation of man's harmful *excess*, present in the animal.

$$[15^1 - 32]$$

The will in itself is free. But every act is determined. We are determined in every act. There are 3 things which must here enter into consideration: Pure possibility, real power,[104] and act. The Laws of these are as follows:

(1) Law of the ideal: All things have ideal existence, which can be in any way conceived.
(2) Law of [the] possible: all things are possible which involve (in themselves) no contradiction.
(3) Law of reality, of all possible things those alone are real[105] which have a sufficient reason for existence.

$$[32^v]$$

The idea of a free determination, that is to say, of an indeterminate indetermination is so unthinkable, so extraordinary that I am[106] astonished to find that any man ever considered it as a real thing.

---

104. ↑real power
105. ↑of all possible things those alone all things are real
106. we are ↑I am

There is no possibility of conciliation in the world of real things between liberty of willing and determinism.

[15¹–51]

Argument against the testimony of consciousness in Free-Will.[107] In post-hypnotic suggestions the patient thinks, that in committing these unmoral actions he[108] is following his own impulse. Tarde.[109]

Therefore, say the determinists, the consciousness of Free-Will[110] is no proof thereof. It may be answered that in this particular case only.

That we may criticize all the better the theory of science in this respect, we must begin with the study of body and of soul, or, rather, of matter and of spirit.

---

107. F[ree]-Will
108. action ~~that~~ he
109. Gabriel de Tarde (1843–1904) was a French sociologist and psychiatrist, and the founder of social psychology and criminality. In Alexander Search's reading notebook [BNP/E3, 144H, 32ʳ], Pessoa lists eleven books by de Tarde: *Criminalité comparée; Les transformations du droit; Les lois sociales; La logique sociale; Les lois de l'imitation; L'opposition universelle; L'opinion et la foule; Les transformations du pouvoir; La philosophie pénale; Études pénales et sociales; Études de la psychologie pénale.*
110. ~~But he is~~ Therefore, say the determinists, the consciousness of F[ree]-W[ill]

Sensation
[51ᵛ]

Besides this Hamon[111] adduces[112] 2 arguments against the possibility of Free-Will. One of them is its contradiction with the Laws of natural causality[113] and of the conservation of matter. Of these the first argument rests on a false basis: the conservation of matter is to-day a matter of doubt. Since the discovery of radium, since the publication of the famous work of Dr. Gustave[114] Le Bon, it has been discussible whether the indestructibility of matter is a truth or is not a truth.

But the argument is worthy of further consideration. It can at least be presented under either of the 2 hypotheses: matter is either indestructible or it is capable[115] of destruction. In the 1ˢᵗ case, □

$$[15^2 - 10^r]$$

Things determined by themselves.

Things determined (by us), by a thing other than themselves.

---

111. Augustin Hamon (1862–1945) was a Belgian sociologist and criminologist. He wrote a book concerning free will entitled *The Universal Illusion of Free Will and Criminal Responsibility*.
112. ↑Besides this Hamon adduces
113. of ↑natural causality
114. G[ustave]
115. is ~~not~~ capable

Things determined to a subject[116] by an object (or objects?).

1. Unknown.
3. Inconceivable.
2. Conceivable.

$$[15^2-35]$$

Genesis of the Idea of Free-Will and genetic critique thereof.

Intellectualization of the material.

Locke (Psychology[117] and moral)

† (indifferent[118] and bad)

Man is a being that reflects on his sensations and by this reflection gives them values.

Intellect the transition 1ˢᵗ between the biologic and the spiritual (moral) worlds.

What is the corresponding point of transition between "inanimate" matter and the biologic[119] world?

motion   (material world)
alteration (Biological world)
           (Spiritual world)

---

116. subj[ect]
117. Psychol[ogy]
118. indiff[eren]t
119. and †ᵗʰᵉ biologic

$[15^3-1\text{ e }2]$

Man has will. Truly he has. Yet let me ask one thing of these philosophers: how do they know that man has will? What is, in their opinion, the criterion of a will? How can we say: this thing possesses a will, that thing does not?

One answer is: by its freedom. This, to me, is no answer at all, for [they] do not admit, nor see a way to admit, the freedom of their faculty. Let us however admit the freedom of the will. Then either freedom is another name for will or it is a property of will. If[120] it be a property of will, it follows that the essence of will is not freedom □

If freedom be the essence of will, since everything is in someway or another limited, nothing at all possesses will.

$[2^r]$

The question is simple. A thing is either free or not free. Either one or the other. There is no mean between these two. There is nothing more free than another thing, unless we are free in a physical sense □

---

120. ~~Wha~~ If

[15A–20]

The anarchist is a product of civilization. Very much as smoke is the product of fire.

The rich with their motor cars.

The Unknown[121] is the reason-for being of the universe. It[122] is no *cause*.

Difference between *cause* and *reason-for-being*. Cause is that by which a phenomenon[123] is, and without which it were not. But if that cause be the phenomenon[124] is.

The Reason-for-being is that by which a phenomenon exists (and its cause); if the phenomenon[125] be not there is a *reason for not being*, but there is no cause.

[20ᵛ]

|The| Sufficient Reason is the sum of the dynamic causes[126] which tend to produce in some direction some effect, *which make an effect as such*.

---

121. ~~God~~ ↑ The Unknown
122. ~~He~~ ↑ It
123. ph[enomenon]
124. ph[enomenon]
125. R[eason]-f[or-]b[eing] is that by which a ph[enomenon] exists (and its cause); if the ph[enomenon]
126. dynamic causes /↑ strength of the causes\

Does the reason-for-being[127] originate anything? Is it the cause of the cause?

Free-Will.

Popular expressions against:
"the best (better) side of a man."
"Character."

[15B¹ – 3]
Psychological[128]

1. Proof taken from witness of conscience.[129]
   a) Stuart Mill's objection.
   b) Spinoza's and Bayle's objection (the so-called direct proof of Free-Will).

Setting apart the awkward idea of infinity in earth, let us observe more clearly this notion. Here again the theory divides: there are either 2 infinite[130] volitions (let it be so) or a universal will manifested in,[131] through, 2 individuals.

---

127. r[eason]-f[or]-b[eing]
128. *Psychologic[al]*.
129. of ~~conse~~ ↑ conscience
130. inf[inite]
131. in ǂ,

Either hypotheses are against free-will. If a Universal[132] Will it is the same in both men; if 2 "absolutes," "infinites" or "indeterminates" in volition they are equal in both men (?). How then does the same cause or 2 like causes (which is the same thing) in the same conditions (the like environment) produce 2 different[133] effects? The answer is obvious: the universal volition[134] (say) in passing through the individual, has determined itself by something in them.

Suppose two men A and B are subjected[135] to a proof, put to the same conditions and that one acts differently from the[136] other. Why is this? Why does it happen? The circumstances, the environment being the same in regard to both men, the actions do not depend on that or, at least, entirely, only upon it. They depend primarily on the two men. Why then should[137] they act differently. Such an act must have a cause.

---

132. Either hypothesis is against free-will. If a Univ[ersal]
133. (~~like~~ the like environment) produce 2 diff[eren]t
134. v[oli]tion
135. ~~put into the same~~ subjected
136. to /↑ from\ the
137. Why ↑then should

[3ᵛ]

The observations[138] and the discussions of introspective psychology are the curse and the bane of argument. Whereas in the observation of a phenomenon of space, that is to say, of a physical phenomenon, a number of intellects can be concerned and, whatever they put out as conclusions, can *observe* to a unity almost, in the old system, and by it, each man and one man is alone responsible for an investigation — for the seeing and for the reasoning thereof. The introspective problems of psychology — those problems, I mean, which are susceptible of solution only by the method of inner self-observation — these are the most difficult of *discussion*.[139] Their method creates the difficulty. Could we look in a spiritual extrospective way[140] into another man's consciousness[141] we would hold the solution of many problems which have tormented mankind for ages.

Psychological arguments.

Walking in the street, too quickly.[142]

---

138. ~~arguments~~ ↑ observings. *We've substituted* "observations" *for* "observings," *since the latter word is likely an authorial lapse.*

139. these ~~problems~~ are the most difficult of *discussion* ↑ all

140. |the| /→ their\ difficulty. Could we look in a spiritual extrospective way /↑ manner\

141. man's consciousness /↑ the c[onsciousness] of another man\

142. <us> mankind for ages. Psychological arguments
    ↓ Walking in the street, too quickly.

[15B¹ – 4 a 4a]

We having[143] admitted the existence of faculties in the human soul, one concept of free-will[144] is alone left us: the notion of liberty of contradicting. It is this: that suppose I have an impulse to steal I can give it my assent or not. According to this theory, the most logical in defence of Free-Will,[145] we have really faculties which when excited predispose us to action, but above them we have the power to act as they bid or not to act.

The notion of liberty is now slightly changed. We do not now[146] claim to be able to choose between 2 opposite things, but, one thing being given as a [4ᵛ] possible to choose to do it or so not to choose.

The dual face of a single thing.[147] Problem takes a weird[148] direction. It is obvious that the power to give[149] or withdraw assent for an impulse cannot be in that impulse which leads only one way, nor in another impulse, or another faculty[150] which leads another way, though not in the opposite way.

---

143. ↑We Having
144. of ~~wil~~ free-will
145. F[ree]-W[ill]
146. not ↑now
147. ~~poss~~ thing
148. ~~strange~~ weird
149. to ~~anoth~~ ↑give
150. another ↑impulse, or another faculty

I shall explain this theory with more clearness. Any man[151] has several faculties in the *possession* of which he differs from other men and [4ʳ] which constitute what is called his character. The old, characterless theory of Free Will can be held no longer. We must allow faculties, and these in different degrees, to make a man's character. But, it is held, behind these faculties there is the will, which gives its assent or not. A man, for instance, with a strong temper has a desire to hit someone, as the violence of his temper [4a] would drive him to do: this is part of the character of the man. Now for the supposed part of the will: the man has the impulse to hit, but he may hit or he may not hit, this, it is asserted, depends on his will, which is free.

$$[15B^2 - 75 \text{ e } 76]$$

true[152]

Comparative freedom of the will.

Higher states of consciousness. Reflexion. Conscience. Effort. (By the higher Conscience[153] is the sentimental part which as primitive exists in degenerates, while the other 2 do not (so to speak).)

These 3 faculties of higher consciousness.

---

151. ↑^Any Man
152. ~~True~~ true
153. Consci[ence]

[76ʳ]
Free-Will

An illusion of the nature of [the] supernatural — immortal things, the application of supernatural to natural.

So is materialism with its infinity of matter.

Overness?

[15B² – 83]
Great Paradox of Free-Will

1. Since we are determined in every action and the quality of our actions linked to the quality of our brain.

2. ☐ [154]

We can only be responsible and free if we are responsible for that brain being as it is. That is to say to be responsible for our state, to be free we must have created our own [self] ourselves. But to create oneself is nonsense (open nonsense; for to create oneself one must exist before one exists — nonsense complete.).

Free-Will is the mode of existence of an Infinite being (if such there be). It may, with incoherence or absurdity, be attributed to God. To man, only absurd and unthinkingly.[155]

---

154. 2. 2. ☐
155. ~~not the~~ unthinkingly

[83ᵛ]

To the question that is suggested: but cannot such soul be an infinite essence □

The answer is no. This by the very definition of infinite. A thing is infinite when nothing else of the same kind exists, for if anything else of the same nature exists, it bounds it and puts a limit to it. A plurality of infinite souls is impossible.

Whereof of finite things, of things of space & of time complete[156] determinism and complete fatalism exists.

The natural world (susceptible as we know of freedom) is either principal, or a manifestation of the psychical world, or side by side with it.
(1) If □, obviously since it is determined, all things are determined, among which psychism, which in this case is a function of matter.
(2) Since the matter represents spirit and shows it further, and since the shown is determined, therefore[157] the thing shown was determined as its essence.
(3) (a) If side by side, any one may be taken, both must be determined [or] else things [will] move not side by side. But (b) both may be [an] expression of *one* reality. But this is entirely unknown.

---

156. con complete
157. ∴ [therefore]

[15B² – 85]

Knowledge of the Future & Free-Will. (Most Important) |*Orsini| in Astronomy.[158] When man shall be able to foresee a |*Society| in Politics.

Knowledge of the Future. Prevision.
 When man shall become fully conscious of determinism then shall he be free.

[15B³ – 13]
Free-Will

(cause is) Force or no-Force
 If no-force it does not act.

If Force it must fight, by measure, a force. (Cf. Herbart).[159]

---

158. Paolo Giordano Orsini (1541-1585) was an Italian nobleman and member of the Roman family of the Orsini, a highly influential princely family in medieval Italy and renaissance Rome that included popes, cardinals, *condottieri* and other political and religious figures. Paolo was the first duke of Bracciano. He is known as one of the patrons of astronomy. Galileo dedicated his 1616 work on the tides to his brother Alessandro.

159. Johann Herbart (1776-1841) was a post-Kantian philosopher. He is considered to be the founder of pedagogy.

For a force does not produce for itself.
(And if one only not the other).
Only *Force* acts for itself.
Energy.

Schopenhauer[160] motion *Sa valeur*.

$$[13^v]$$

Common notion of place.[161]

Like the cells
 That, by dividing, multiply.

Le spectre immonde de la mort.

But bound in chest and with gilt edges.

Haeckek's *monistic dualism*.
 Argument[162] of Unity. Pass to O = not pass.

---

160. Schop[enhauer]
161. ~~Which~~
 Common not[ion] of place
162. Arg[umen]t

Push this argument to the end.

Smith and Jones.

Hypocrite.

[15B³–22]
Hypothesis of Free-Will:

The so-called free-will is the result of consciousness and action. Thus (ordinarily unconscious)[163] action and consciousness becomes in seeming free.

Seems free by passing through consciousness.

Similarly in intellectualization.

Similarly "*Logique du sentiment.*"

---

163. (↑ ordinarily unconscious

[15B³ – 91]
Origin of the Error of Free-Will

The Synthetic nature of Consciousness, making one of many, yet not properly a whole.

[15B⁴ – 8]

The emptiness of the theory of free-will has even never been sufficiently exposed. Of the philosophers who have dealt with it, the idealists and semi-idealists have seen clearly into the problem but have wrapped their thoughts in language so philosophical that the reader has no equally clear idea of the nature of the discussion. On the other side, the scientists, who see clearly into nothing because their talent is observing [164] — the scientists, I say, content themselves with denying the theory and swearing at it, without the fragment of a clear idea as to what free-will means or as to [165] what it does not mean.

———

The practical side of the problem everybody can see; seeing this is what the scientists consider [166] having a clear idea of the problem.

---

164. because ~~they~~ their ~~observe too much~~ ↑ talent is observing
165. an ᶜˡᵉᵃʳ idea ~~of~~ ↑ ᵃˢ ᵗᵒ what free-will means ~~and of~~ ↑ ᵒʳ ᵃˢ ᵗᵒ
166. scientists ~~call~~ ↑ consider

ON FREE WILL

[8ᵛ]

I hope to prove by the arguments that follow that free-will is incompatible with either of the hypotheses. If the soul be simple, free-will is unthinkable. If the soul be composed, free-will is impossible.

(Here follow the arguments otherwhere written down).

The problem of free-will is bound up entirely with the question as to whether what is called the human soul be simple or be composed. It is assumed that if the simpleness of the soul be proved, its freedom to act is consequent.[167]

[15B⁴ – 17 a 18]

Now the explanation of how man came to conceive his will as indetermined must be given.[168]

To refute is only part of dialectics; explanation is the other; where all arguments have been used the doubt still remains that there may not be an argument to destroy them. But when error, besides being refuted, is explained, when it is shown[169] how error is error, then,

---

167. is ~~proved~~ consequent
168. given. ~~Because~~
169. is ~~p~~ shown

the refutation is complete. It is a poor philosophy which covers itself only with arguments and never with impulsion; such metaphysics has been, and the tendency it has shown has been to discard ideas[170] for terms, arguments with terms, all hollowness, all, where all is clear, all deduced, all †, but nothing intimately comprehended or perceived. The metaphysicians who argue of nature[171] is generally possible to understand nature _ _ _ _

We are then brought face to face[172] with the question of error. How is error possible? To those who deal in terms and are conscious-agents of hollowness it may seem a strange problem. Nevertheless it is of importance, as all problems are, being all part of one problem, linked together as blood and bone.[173]

Plato _ _ _

[17ᵛ]

Now first it is clear that in error two things are needed to make it error: that something should be true, that something should be false: a principle of truth and a principle of error. I mean we must determine what is it that makes us see truth, what is it that leads into error.

---

170. discard ~~its~~ ideas
171. of ~~God~~ nature
172. face /↑ heart\ to face /↑ heart\
173. and bone /↑ flesh\

ON FREE WILL

Let us reason abstractly, let us examine the case in the[174] correct, in an example, in an indubitable error. We may thus |*sign| the process.

Let us take a very simple error, that, for instance, of saying that 5 and 4 and 3[175] make 11 (instead of 12). How can this originate? In 1 of 3 things: either in a misapprehension of fact; or in a false[176] reasoning (in adding up — i.e., a false manner of adding) or in both things.

The question is no sooner asked than answered, solved. The process of adding cannot lead us away for the process of adding is one in all cases; if I use to attempt to add by multiplying, by comparison, the _ _ _ _ _ _ Now since this is so, no man can then be erred in the process and also put together. If I see clearly that 5 is 5, that 4 is 4, that 3 is 3, I can't say that 5 plus 4 plus 3 is[177] equal to 11. It is only if I could say 4 as 3, by mistake, that I am faced with that error.

[18ʳ]
(Third Case goes first — before addition)

Again, I see a |*vice|; no one else in the case which is presupposed sees it. I am in an error.[178] How?

---

174. in a ↑the
175. make ↑and 3
176. f false
177. I saw see clearly that 4 ↑5 is 4 ↑5, that 4 is 4, that 3 is 3 I can't say that 5 and ↑plus 4 and ↑plus 3 is is
178. in ↑an error

Now we have in the 1ˢᵗ case (that of the hallucination) an error of sensation; in the second (addition) an error of intellect. That is why the hallucination-case went[179] first.

|Error is then the personal interpretation of an impersonal thing, the particular interpretation[180] of a general thing. All forms of error fall into this definition.|

No one draws a wrong conclusion from facts because[181] facts do not exist, but only interpretations, perceptions of facts. What each man in error[182] does is to draw legitimate conclusions from misinterpreted facts.

Personality, sensation — is the principle of error.

$$[15B^4 - 74^r]$$

An individual[183] A, who is drowning and is helped by B, paralyses B's movements by holding convulsively onto his arms. Hamon gives this act as the example of an *unconscious* act.

(It is an act without the assent of the will, as older philosophers might say) — What does this mean?

Free-Will. I and II.

Definition of Crime. III and IV.

---

179. only the ~~first case~~ hallucination-case ~~went~~ ↑ went
180. interpret[ati]on
181. ∴ [because]
182. man ↑ in error
183. ~~Bartholomeus.~~
    An individual

[22 – 18ʳ]

To say the will (infinite) acts on matter, which is finite, is to talk nonsense. The infinite cannot work or act [184] upon the finite. An infinite will does not act at all; it is, very simply, a will-in-power, more simply still, it is a *power*. The moment there is an act, this will-in-power becomes will-in-act, becomes determined as will-in-act, is finite no longer.

[23 – 13 – 16]

The Human soul is either simple or composed: that is to say, either it is the whole and the same soul which thinks, feels, desires, calculates, perceives; or each faculty or manifestation of the soul □ or the soul is [185] made up of several faculties separate and distinct from one another, which have each its own function, and nothing to do with the function of the others. The creation of unity is merely assumed by consciousness, in this latter case.

[14ʳ]

The soul may be composed in 2 ways.
 a) In nature, as a body skin, flesh, and bone, a case of good and ally □ [186]

---

184. or /↑ nor\ act
185. the ↑ soul is
186. ↑ a case of ~~nerve~~ ↑ good and ~~corporal~~ alby

b) In degree, as a number of □ which denote[187] one unity, one, ten, one hundred and so on.
c) In both,[188]
   a) In the first case, the intellectual faculties, for instance would be distinct from the animal propensities and thus these can be no combating of this theory as[189] we combated that of the *simple soul*. This[190] theory is against the unity of the soul.
   b) In this case, these would be[191] really a unity in the soul, but a kind of degree makes it of the nature of composed. Thus, in this theory, the intellectual faculties would be a superior aggregation of the particles or small things which form, for instance, the animal faculties. I do not know[192] that this theory exists, but I have to consider it, inasmuch as it comes logically into my discussion.

[15ʳ]

Now whichever of these two theories[193] we accept, free-will is inconsistent with both.

---

187. a) If in nature, denote
188. c) In nature and degree.
    c) In both, as the legs and arms, stomach and heart of a body.
189. as ↑ as
190. But This
191. unity is ↑ would be
192. Of this I do not know
193. theories /↑ hypotheses\

ON FREE WILL

a) if the soul be simple, then its faculties, being merely manifestations, of the same thing[194] have all the same nature.

If they have the same nature, then the intellectual faculties have the same nature as, for instance, the appetitive or the regulative faculties.

From this results the strange conclusion that, if we own a man possible to make himself good or evil, we own him also able at will to make himself a genius or an idiot, intellectually a Kant or a grocer's assistant.[195] And this conclusion is manifestly false.

b) Let the human soul be composed; it[196] may be composed in □ ways. Firstly, the human faculties may be the same in composition, in fact, the same in nature, but different from a material localization (this is the theory of the Phrenologists, according to whom the faculties have the same composition[197] — i.e., the cerebral mass — but different manifestations, according to their position in the head.).[198] Cf. Plato:

> part of soul in head.
> part of soul in breast.
> part of soul in stomach.

---

194. its ~~manifestations~~ ↑ faculties, being merely manifestations, ~~are~~ ↑ of the same thing

195. *Transcribed exactly as it is in the manuscript.*

196. ~~If~~ ↑ Let the human soul be composed; ~~then~~ it

197. comp[osition]

198. their position in the head). /↓ part of the head they occupy\

[15ᵛ]

Secondly, the human soul may be composed of faculties of [199] entirely different nature, of different material position.[200] For instance, Plato's theory (verso).

In the first case, the will, being a manifestation of the human mind, and all other [201] faculties, e.g., the intellective being susceptible of degrees, it is evident that the will itself is susceptible of degrees.

But could not the will be external to these, independent of them, powerful (or consciousness) over all? If so, then the power would extend (as in the case of the simple soul) to intellect and the same impossible conclusion should be attained.[202]

[16ʳ]

Thirdly, the human soul may be composed, as we may say, by degrees. Suppose the mind formed of one kind of monads [203] or spiritual atoms; make out that a small grouping of these produces the lower faculties, and so on, progressively, the intellect being the highest aggregation. I do not think any one has ever had this theory, neither

---

199. of ↑ faculties of
200. nature. † of different material filiation
201. and ↑ all other
202. conclusion ↑ should be attained
203. of ↑ one kind of monads

shall I call it[204] mine; I have put it down here merely because it comes naturally into the discussion.

Fourthly, the human soul may be composed both in nature and in degree; supposing, I mean to say, agglomerations of particles of different nature, rising in power, or, perchance, purifying itself to oneness and in composition, as in the intellectual faculties.

[16ᵛ]

Consider the moral sense. Simple.
Composed
- In material position
- In degree
- In very nature
- In nature & in degree
- In nature and material[205] position.[206]

[23 – 17ʳ]

The human soul[207] is declared to be simple.

If it be simple, then all human faculties have the same nature.

---

204. neither is ↑ shall I call it
205. mat[eria]l
206. *At the end of the page one reads*: ignoratio elenchi ignoratio elenchi. Elenchi.
207. human ↑ soul

If all human faculties have the same nature, the intellectual faculties have the same nature as, for instance, the motive faculties.

If this be so, the other faculties vary in the same way as the intellectual; and it is as idiotic to hold that a man can be good or bad, at will, or that he can be clever[208] or stupid, a genius or an idiot at pleasure.

[23 – 26 a 27]

All evil comes from the sentiment of obstacle, or, seeking deeper, by the sentiment of limitation. All evil, all unhappiness is in being limited, in having a bound. All unhappiness is a sentiment of our deficiency.

One argument against: the sentiment of my excessive viciousness, for instance, which is the sentiment of an excess, gives pain. — *Answer*: No[,] what gives pain is the sentiment of our lack of power to control it. The man who is vicious purely and wishes not to control this viciousness, is not unhappy at all. Therefore that excess, same in him as in me, is not the cause of unhappiness. If I am unhappy it is not because of it.

All pain is the result of limitation. The poet is [...] [26ᵛ] thought becomes imperfect in words. The thinker is unhappy when there is a problem he cannot solve: sentiment of obstacle, of limitation.

---

208. ~~good~~ clever

Space and time are the conditions of existence,²⁰⁹ of pain, of action.

Relative freedom attenuates our pain. But the selfish, the egoistic are happy. Now what is selfishness? The sentiment of self-sufficiency,²¹⁰ of self-perfection. But as nobody, as nothing is perfect in the universe, a sentiment of self-perfection, is a sentiment of the perfection²¹¹ of an imperfection, that is, such a sentiment, being false, is itself an imperfection.

Limitation is therefore the sort not only of all unhappiness but also of all evil.

[27ʳ]

Man is either free or determined. Indetermination has no degrees.

Before this that²¹² evil consists in limitation, consequently in personality, the theory of the immortality of the soul cannot²¹³ be considered as true, neither as cheerful nor satisfying. Personality is always limitation, however ideal or metaphysical.²¹⁴

---

209. ~~ide rea~~ existence
210. ~~myself~~ ↑ self-sufficiency
211. of ↑ the perfection
212. this ~~theory~~ that
213. soul ~~need not b~~ cannot
214. satisfying. → Penalty is always limitation, however ideal or metaphysical.

Regarding life as a reality[215] of their ill — reasoned dualism, the Christian[216] philosophers are materialistic in wishing to perpetuate a material state in a world which is not material.

The things in which the greatest pleasure lies are those which we regard as nearest to the unlimited.[217] Imagination, juvenile impulse, enthusiasm, etc.

[27ᵛ]

All the loftiest, all the noblest poetical conceptions are strivings after the unlimited.

[23 – 29ʳ]

Psychological automatism. The natural form of human action.
Human consciousness the centralization of the automatism of our faculties[218] in the mind.
"The beautiful is the beautiful." All primitive ideas are indefinable […] if we think to define them, it is a pure illusion. They are always[219] defined by themselves. Thus plurality, space, time, etc.

---

215. a /(one)\ reality
216. they Christian
217. the infinite. ↑ unlimited.
218. o[ur] faculties
219. al[ways]

"Time is the order of durations." But duration supposes time.

Critique of argument of determinism. "True; I cannot think as I will, nor be a genius or a fool at pleasure. But I can think it possible to live without eating, or to jump from here to the moon. That is to say, I can choose my thoughts, wild or not, within the sphere of necessity imposed by my general nature. Thus, I may be incapable of acts of great benevolence, but [220] I may be able to choose between giving a counterfeit shilling to anyone or not giving it." This answer is false, rests on a false basis.

What is not indeterminate is determinate; there is no avoiding this.

What is not free is unfree; this cannot be denied. Necessity and freedom cannot be found together.

Matter is a shell of properties. Spirit is the matter thereof.

[23 – 30 a 31]

If it can be proved that free-will cannot exist it is not only Free-Will that is touched but likewise [221] the immortality of the soul.

---

220. ~~or~~ but
221. only F[ree]-W[ill] that is touched ~~by~~ ↑but likewise

Besides, either the body & the soul are two distinct and separate things or they are one. Either the soul is the form of the body, or the body is the manifestation of the soul.

If the soul be the form of the body, _ _ _

If the body be the manifestation of the soul, it is evident that when the manifestation is dispelled the thing manifested also goes, since it is not very clear how a thing now manifests itself and again does not.

[30ᵛ]

The vegetative soul principle of existence.
 The animal soul principle of □
 The *νοῦς* principle of motion, thought.

[31ʳ]

Man, being an intellectual animal, transforms sensations by virtue of that intellect. Thus physical love is transformed into "marital affection" and the term "purity *in love*" is introduced. The brutal & natural action of blow for blow is given a value and transformed into "valour,"[222] "courage" already in a higher sense. In the same way it is natural that physical liberty should become, by intellect, moral liberty, "free-will." All the question then appears to be [is] this: is the mutation of the point of view correspondent to a legitimate change in the thing? Is not the question all here?

---

222. a "valour"

[31ᵛ]

There is one thing to be noticed. It is the notion of value that man (and man alone) puts upon things. For the animal, courage, cowardice[223] are not, one good, the other bad, one noble, the other ignoble. They have no value at all. To[224] man they wear a moral face.

If moral liberty exists it is here that we must find it, it is of necessity bound up with this.

Now there are several things here which must be explained. One is the appearance of moral sense.

[23 – 48 a 50]

Consider the extraordinary dualism which man presents of *natural* and of *moral* sentiment. Nature is "red in foot and claw"; the law of nature is selfishness. Man, indeed, acts most often — most often, in truth — according to this law of nature. Man, deny it not, is a selfish being, however natural he be in so being. But man when postulating his own moral rules never sincerely builds them upon egotism but upon altruism, and thus, in an advanced ethics, we are unnatural, we are in opposition to nature. Whence do we draw this idea of altruism which is not in nature? What has this to do with the "idea of Free-Will" of M. Fouillée?

---

223. ~~fear~~ ↑ cowardice
224. ~~In~~ ↑ To

[49ʳ]

The idea of free-will, in my opinion, has its rise in the application to the moral world of the primitive and natural idea of *physical liberty*. This application, this analogy is unconscious; and it is also false. It is, I repeat, one of those unconscious errors which we make, one of those false reasoning [in] which we so often and so naturally indulge. Schopenhauer has pointed out that [225] the primitive notion of liberty is "absence of obstacles," a purely physical notion. And in our human conception of liberty the notion holds. No man considers an idiot, a madman (to be)[226] responsible. Why? Because he conceives something in the brain as an obstacle to true judgement.

[49ᵛ]

Idea of liberty a purely metaphysical idea.

The primary idea is the idea of responsibility, which is only the application of the idea of cause, by the reference of an effect to its Cause. "That man hits me; I hit him in defence." "That man struck that other man and killed him. I saw him. That man is the *cause* of the other's death." All this is perfectly true.

Thus we see that the idea of free-will[227] is not a primi-

---

225. pointed out — I need hardly say with how much subtlety — that
226. holds ↑considers an idiot, a madman ↑(to be)
227. lib free-will

tive idea at all; that responsibility, founded on a legitimate yet ignorant application of the principle of causality, is the really primitive[228] idea.

In the beginning man is not conscious of any but physical liberty. In the beginning there is no such metaphysical state of mind. The idea of liberty is come by reason, is metaphysical & therefore susceptible of error.

[50ʳ]

Again popular opinion, as we see by this, puts the real element of moral liberty in judgement, in consideration, in the power to perceive, to discern good and ill and to discuss them mentally. But this statement[229] is false. The popular conception is this: that *judgement* is that which considers a thing, deciding whether it be right or wrong. In the popular opinion it is this faculty that tells us that a thing is good or bad; it is, they think, the element of good in us. The people[230] thinks that if I see by this that an action is bad and I do it nevertheless, I am guilty of evil. The idea of moral liberty is not in any way primitive, not even[231] of to-day in the popular mind, or, hypothetically, in any cultured mind which might ignore the question entirely. It is an idea came by reason,

---

228. ~~and~~ primitive
229. this ~~as~~ statement
230. ~~crow~~ people
231. ~~much less~~ ↑ not even

a philosophical idea. Primitively [50ᵛ] there is neither a sense of moral liberty nor a sense of being determined. It [232] is idle to think that a savage has any sense of moral liberty.

Man is perfectly an animal and the only primitive sense in this case is the sense of physical freedom: "I can do what I will."

Of this there is of course no doubt. So long as I am not imprisoned, nor (en)chained, nor paralytic, nor hindered by any physical obstacle, I am *free*: I can do what I will. "But can I will what I will and will nothing else?" The great question is all here.

Now this primitive unconsciousness, which way does it rather point (more):[233] to free-will or to determinism?

[23 – 51 a 53]
On Free-Will
Argument of Consciousness:

Example: "I am going to meet a man with whom I must have a discussion and I wonder and fear what may happen, if I may not lose my temper and became involved in a fight." Now the first thing to be noted here is that the individual who makes these reflections has a temper. A man who had not would not make these considerations if he had not the power to get into a rage. The supposed argument then is changed. It is no longer: "I feel in me

---

232. of ↑ being determinism/↑ ed\. W̶ It
233. does it ↑ rather point m̶o̶r̶e̶ ↑ (more)

the power to do either of two things"; it is now: "of two things *I have in me* I feel the power to do one." And this is true, perfectly true. It is the Law of internal contradiction, the first law of (all) truth: Anything can exist, may [51ᵛ] come to be so long as it involves no contradiction." Thus the man with no temper does not consider the possibility of doing harm: such a possibility is in contradiction with his own character, involves contradiction, and, breaking the law [234] is not possible. It cannot happen at all. An act needs a power of the kind: *ex nihilo nihil.*

On the other hand the impulsive, hot-tempered man fears himself. He doubts whether he will be firm enough to keep back [235] his rage. More clearly and with greater truth: he is uncertain as to which of the 2 faculties he possesses, violence and firmness, will [236] conquer in the end. He ignores, moreover, the circumstances, the conditions in which they are to be tried. He is ignorant that is of the future environment. The other man may fire him with certain [52ᵛ] expressions, may keep him still with others, guarded and cautious. Were you to say to this man: "so-and-so will, in the discussion, insult you to-day." The hot-tempered man will answer you, if he be sincere: "Then I shall get into a fury." He knows it well — he will. Here is the complete determination of future action, the environment (in this case, the insults) being known.

---

234. law̶
235. keep back /(cheek)\
236. i̶s̶ will

Indeterminists urge commonly that it is impossible to predetermine, to prophesize the actions of any man. Far from impossible, when the character and the environment are well known,[237] the action is known. How could it not be, since it is a product of both? Seven and five known, who cannot say they make twelve?

[52^v]

A man ignores often how he will act. Were we free we could say: "I shall act thus," and do so. A certain young soldier goes to battle wondering whether his courage will fail him or not. Here is clearly either ignorance of himself, his courage never having been tried, or ignorance of the true nature of the environment, though never having had his courage tested in this way. There is no room, I believe, for an indeterminist explanation. The tired general goes to battle knowing that he will *not* feel fear: complete knowledge of himself and of the nature of the environment. The two □ completely known their sum cannot fail to be known likewise.

[53^r]

Having come thus far we are now and at this point made to face another problem, which is important and not without interest. It is contained in this: "how have we

---

237. are $^{↑\text{well}}$ known

the idea of liberty if such liberty does not exist? How do we believe ourselves free if we are determined in our every act?"

There are several philosophers who have written on this point. Their aim has been chiefly to conciliate determinism and responsibility. What reason there is for doing this I do not know. Is it that they do not wish science to take from governments and from powers the holy and sacred right of and reason for inflicting penalties upon men? Or is it a certain fear of the new, a certain remnant of respect for the old and warmly cherished ideas which are generally, if not entirely, wrong?

[53ᵛ][238]

Now the idea of liberty is either legitimate or it is not. If it be an idea, truly and purely a simple idea, it is, *ipso facto*, legitimate, and liberty is a truth.[239] Or on the other hand it[240] is only by name an idea, that is, an intuition, of the nature of those of time, of space, of colour, or, still better of those of good and of beautiful. In this latter case since it is not an intuition, it must be the result[241] of reasoning.

---

238. [53ᵛ]
~~Johannes Scot Erigenes: "De Naturæ divisione."~~
~~De "divina pedistinatione."~~
239. truth. /(fact).\
240. Or ↑ on the other hand it
241. case if ↑ since it be ↑ is not an intuition, it must be a ↑ the result

We shall now consider both these theories.

In the 1st place, free-will has not the characteristic quality of intuition,[242] simplicity. An intuition cannot be defined. What colour is, what space is, we cannot say; if we define them, we do so wrongly and in terms of the thing defined.[243]

[23 – 79]

Good and the influence[244] of it on the will.

Suppose a man to act wrongly.[245] Now this man either has a moral or has not.

If he have not he acts wrongly only to other men, and in ignorance.

Here, *peccatum ab errore.*

If he have, how is it that he commits a wrong deed? If he does nay, rather, since he does, and since he has a moral sense, either that moral sense does not act, or, if it act, it is susceptible of being overruled.

The 1st hypothesis is false: a power that does not act is nothing at all, consists[246] but in the supposition, in words void of sense.

---

242. ~~liberty~~ free-will has not the characteristic quality of ↑intuition,
243. thing ~~we must~~ defined
244. the ~~idea~~ influence
245. ~~rightly~~ wrongly
246. ~~is~~ consists

[79ᵛ]

As to the 2ⁿᵈ hypothesis, it appears, since the 1ˢᵗ hypothesis is false, that either the moral sense varies in intensity from man to man, that, therefore, the moral sense is susceptible of degrees (therefore[247] material), or that it is present in some men and absent in others.

[26 - 90 a 92]

I do not comprehend how predestination can be conciliated with free-will. I know that God as conceived in the philosophy of the churches cannot but be held as knowing all things. The future is known then to him as the present. But, with God, to know is not as with us. With us, to know is to see what we saw not before, we *receive* instruction. But[248] with God — with the God of the Churches — to know is identical with to do, else there is no unity in his nature. If God[249] knows our sins it is because he makes them. Cf. Aristotle's hypothesis of God's ignorance of world. These[250] contradictions are very common in the philosophy of the churches. The Christian God is an infant's riddle — it has an answer but no sense.

---

247. ∴ [therefore]
248. ~~With~~ ↑But
249. [g|G]od
250. ↓ Cf. Arist[otle] hypothesis of God's ignorance of world These

[90ᵛ]

☐ the people, stupid & useful,²⁵¹ deserving of pity and of love.

Immortality is a higher thing than death. It does not represent an advance to relinquish this dogma of the churches. To understand its reason, to know why it exists, to comprehend it — this would be the true advance. After dogmatic affirmation should come not his negation, but comprehension. And these or perhaps abstract, or conciliate negation or affirmation with a reason. A wilful²⁵² accep[ta]tion of mortality, without conditions and without longing [is] a stigma of retrocess[ion].²⁵³

Those who let drop this idea, however they cover themselves with the cloak of science, have beneath it but the skeleton of the vertebrate.

[91ʳ]

Christianity here is false; it attempts to reconstruct part of the material world, leaving out & forgetting the other.

---

251. ~~useless~~ ↑ useful

252. ↓ To understand its reason, to know why it exists, to comprehend it — this would be the true advance. After dogmatic affirmation should come not ↑ his negation, but comprehension. And these → or perhaps abstract, or conciliate negation or affirmation with a reason. A wilful

253. ~~is a stigma of degeneration~~ a stigma of retrocess

Buddhism is more profound. It is a better consolation for the soul. I read of the 4 sublime truths, not shaken[254] by fear, but thrilled for their sublimeness. That wiping out of the world entire, that *nirvanâh*, world of consolation and of not-pain, there is no soul but yearns for it. A sleep of death without dreams, a ceasing of personality — we can desire nothing better, nor wish for anything more deep. Yet I do not like.

Friar Maurice, the madman.[255]

Personality is the place of evil; the heart the sanctuary[256] of pain. We do not desire men's good but their evil, when we wish them to be immortal.

[92ʳ]

It is often said, with words that fill the mouth, that Christianity is a sad thing, that its ethics is sad, and that it gives us a sad view of life. We all know what this means. It means that Christianity does not sanction vice, that it does not allow our passions their full scope, that it makes us weary of living[257] by condemning our pleasures. Oh, we understand well those words and know what sentiment has inspired them!

---

254. not (~~with~~) shaken
255. seep. → Yet I do not like. Friar Maurice, the madman.
256. the ~~pla~~ sanctuary
257. of ~~life~~ ↑ living

In Christianity, true, there are things to be condemned. The theory of free-will, the horrible doctrine of hell — all these things are bad, primitive, immoral. It is not that Christianity saddens this life, but that saddens the world beyond.

[92ᵛ]

It gives us a bad finiteness here upon earth and shows to us, beyond this, the dreadful possibility of an eternity of pain. The shudder of Pascal cannot be repressed. Not the most dogmatic pessimism ever shook us with such affright.

Book [258]
Friar
<u>Maurice</u>

[55E – 4]

I had first determined to call free-will an illusion, but this assertion I have changed, seeing that practically few of us believe in free-will, and none act as if it existed. Free-will is [259] but a fallacy. I cannot but allow that many good and sincere men have believed in the existence of this liberty. And many other men who may have been good,

---

258. B[oo]k
259. ↑but is

but also were certainly not sincere, have defended the[260] theory with great ferocity. But even sincere and good[261] men may be a little stupid, and may not have [4ᵛ] reason on their side, while, on the other hand, ferocious men are almost always in the wrong. Few men fight as fiercely as the man who defends a lie, his as somebody else's; harm commonly it is his or he has made it his own.

[133C – 15]
Contradictions

Free-Will and Predestination.[262]
    Free-Will and Finality in nature.

[144J – 45ᵛ a 49ʳ]

Free-Will exactly a theory included in dualism and specially arising (as principle doctrine) from[263] the seeing of how rapid the spirit passes from ill to good, how it changes …

    (analysis psychological)

    Now this change of mind is characteristically hysteric. Another thing to prove that dualism is linked to hysteria.

---

260. defended ~~with grea~~ the
261. ~~great~~ ↑ good
262. Fr[ee]-Will and Predest[ination]
263. arising ↑ (as principle doctrine) from

For the dualist the world has no value as by non-spirit — For the idealist it has a value, it is the manifestation of spirit. A manifestation: something that means more than it is — here the mania of doubt.

[46ʳ]

Spiritualisation of the material, so to speak.

Free-Will

An exterior thing strikes only one tendency: the action is simple. Danger comes, and there is no reason to remain, suppose, not even, honour, or self-esteem; the sentiment of fear is hit,[264] this sentiment only, and I flee. Such is a simple action.

But suppose that[265] to my sentiment of fear my sentiment of fear of ridicule is hit;[266] the case becomes complex. I have either to flee (as bid me my sentiment of fear) or to remain [46ᵛ] (as imposes my sentiment of ridicule). All the problem lies in this: do these motives *choose themselves*, that is to say, is there in them in regard to each other a quantitative strength, by which one predominates over the other? Or, on the other side, is there a thing superior to them, a will, to *choose*, in the true sense of the word,

---

264. I flee the sentiment of fear is stru hit
265. such ↑ that
266. str hit

between them? The question, I repeat, is all here? This will cannot choose in view of such, etc., therefore will choose in view of itself therefore does not exist.[267]

We will begin from the beginning. We will take[268] the simple case first. That my sentiment of fear being alone hit and *no other*. Better; we will [47ʳ] reject this example and take one where all is much clearer. Suppose it is the sentiment of sex that is[269] hit by an exterior excitation, that sentiment alone, as is easy to happen. The action that will result will be inevitably an impulse of[270] the sexual kind, an impulse to copulate.

But suppose the man in whom this impulse comes is[271] at that moment *épuisé*, what then? What checks him from sexual action? Consideration for his health? He may have no such consideration. Timidity, lack of lust, honour, etc., etc.? We suppose he has none such. The answer is [47ᵛ] therefore[272] obvious: the very sentiment hit, being already satiated, will react and kill itself, so to speak. Here we find a sentiment checks itself. Here we perceive a duality where there was none apparent.[273]

---

267. here? ← imp[ortan]t → This will cannot choose in view of such etc. ∴ [therefore] will choose in view of itself ∴ [therefore] does not exist.

268. We will /↑ shall\ begin from the beginning. We will /↑ shall\ take

269. Suppose ~~my~~ ↑ it is the sentiment of sex ↑ that is

270. ~~to~~ of

271. ~~has~~ ↑ is

272. ∴ [therefore]

273. ~~What was~~ Here we perceive a duality where there was none apparent[?|.]

What is the name of this? Let us see first if it is general. Let us consider the animals[274] love [rather] than man. Is this. In animals the case is very simple. The animal satisfies its sexual instinct (if it can) when such is excited[275] and then calms down. Instinct and sexual excitation are in[276] the animal proportional to sexual power. Some animals are sexually more ardent, others less, and these are all [48ʳ] sexually excitable in the direct ratio of their power.[277] There is no animal to which could happen that case of the □ youth who after right a both committed masturbation of this, desires of this soon after.[278] It occurs at once to ask —why? Why is disparate[279] and disproportion of desire and of power peculiar to man. Temptation, free-will, etc. I consider no answers. At many actions is will analogous [to] the matter. We notice of course that man, normally, is as the animal.[280]

From[281] the considerations that precede the reader will have taken this, that normally one[282] sentiment alone, if excited, contains in itself its own control. What explanation is then for this [48ᵛ] phenomenon?

---

274. ~~Is it general?~~ Let us see first if it is general. Let us consider the
275. s excited ~~an~~ animal
276. ~~ex~~ sexual excitation is /↑ are\ in
277. their ~~ardency~~ ↑ power
278. desires of this ~~essecen~~ soon after
279. ~~cannot man be~~ is disparate
280. matter. → We notice of course that man, normally, is as the animal.
281. ~~The~~ From
282. that ↑ normally one

In the old though shortest way of seeing there were[283] considered two kinds of "liberties": that of □ as to love or to hate, and that of □ as to love, or not-to-love. It is the second of these that is here involved.[284] Are we free to love or not-to-love?

§ Let us consider. Does the beloved who yields to sexual impulse beyond his own power manifest a disease of *entire self-control*? No, for a disease of *entire* self-control would have rendered him incapable of being long[285] before. He is then right to a lack of control in *that* sentiment (that of sexuality) *alone*. Let [49ʳ] us suppose so (for we may be also with control in others). What conclusion is clearly to be drawn from here? This, that every *sentiment has its own control*. When forced to excess every sentiment is uncontrolled.[286]

But, you will ask, in view of what does control not. Since the control is closely inherent to a sentiment [it] is neither that of fear of ridicule, nor of honour, love of men[287] for health etc., etc., but simply a control and no more?

---

283. old ↑though shortest way of seeing there were /↑are\
284. here pr involved
285. made reduced him incapable of being before long
286. *control.* ↓ When forced to excess every sentiment is uncontrolled.
287. ↑Since Is closely ↑the control essential ↑inherent to a sentiment is neither that of fear of ridicule, nor of from ↑honour and love of men

Struggle of an impulse in itself (1).

Struggle of 2 or[288] more low impulses among themselves (2).

Struggle of 1 or more low and instinct (or more high impulses (3)).

Since high impulses do not conflict[289] or contradict each other.

Evolution of inhibition.

---

288. 2 ~~va~~ ↑or
289. ~~fight together~~ conflict

III – On the Idea of Responsibility

[23 – 54 a 57]

On the Idea of Responsibility

In the middle of the human brain, in those wonderful organs in which [290] is centralized the nervous system, which form therefore human consciousness........ In these and nowhere else is the idea of Myself. We are bound to admit that this idea is allied to the activity of these organs, because they are the most central in the human brain.

Around these are, must be — we have proved it — the central seats of the various passions and of the various emotions, which are all of them susceptible [291] of degrees. The consciousness of the activity, and of the possibility of the activity of these is the consciousness of our own personality. There is no mystery in it; everything is quite clear.

[54ᵛ]

Now all human activity is of [292] these various seats of those diverse passions and emotions. Their centraliza-

---

290. organs ↑ⁱⁿ which
291. are ↑ᵃˡˡ ᵒᶠ ᵗʰᵉᵐ susceptible
292. ↑ⁱˢ of

tion is the idea of their unification, of their unity. There is no centre of personality in a positive meaning of the word "centre." What there is is a centralization.

Now the centralization of theses emotions and, consequently, of their activity, means the consciousness of this personality, that is, of these emotions and passions[293] as *cause*. There is this, and there is no more.

Consciousness of my Self as Cause — this is the first element of the pseudo-idea of responsibility. But notice especially, notice well how misleading, how false this conception is.

[55ʳ]
Responsibility

Notice that the real notion of my emotion[294] as cause, *centralized*, seems to be, in the mind, the notion of *the*[295] *centre* as cause, the notion of myself as Cause. Here then is the true, the real Cause of the[296] pseudo idea of Free-Will: the transmutation of the act of the emotions which[297] are mine into the acts of *myself*. True, my self is my emotions, centralized, but in emotions is the basis of myself and not in the centralization[298] of them.

---

293. personality ↓ *that is, of these emotions and passions*
294. emotions
295. of a ↑ *the*
296. Here ↑ *then* is the true, the real Cause ~~for~~ ↑ *of* the
297. ↑ *the act of the* emotions ~~acts into~~ which
298. my ↑ *in* emotions ~~are~~ ↑ *is the basis of* myself and not ↑ *in* the centralization

If my emotions be decentralized, as happens in instinctive acts, in customary[299] acts, in sleep, in a state of hypnosis — still they [55ᵛ] can act. But a centralization, in itself, is an abstraction, is nothing. The emotions are the principal things. The centralization of nothing is nothing.

It is urgent for me here to point out the sovereign importance of this principle. It is the basis of the human, too human, dogmas of the immortality of the soul, of its freedom, of its perfect simplicity. The stupendous realization of an abstraction which consists in elevating a mere *centralization* of emotions, which has a reality *by* them and *in* them, and only in so far as they are there all centralized, [56ʳ] in elevating this into a reality, into a personality — this is the lowly and feeble basis of the most rooted dogmas, of many and many of the most transcendent[300] speculations.

Besides the refutation, by the search for origins, of these traditional dogmas, this principle — not to say, this discovery — gives us a new method in the science of psychology. Psychology ceases to treat and to consider the individual soul, very naturally, because this does not exist.

The problem[301] is no longer [56ᵛ] the problem of body and soul,[302] but the problem of matter and of energy,

---

299. in ha customary
300. transcendant, *in the original. Possible authorial lapse.*
301. True psy The problem
302. of soul

of matter and (of) spirit. The[303] character of mystery which rested upon the human soul[304] was the natural outcome of the realisation of an abstraction. Our psychology must be henceforth the[305] psychology of the cell, and our chief inquiry into how colonies of cerebral molecules when in vibration are associated with a sensation, such as that of fear.[306] We must cultivate, as Lange[307] enjoined us to do, a "psychology without soul."

Do not believe that by this elimination of spirit mystery disappears [57ʳ] from the world and everything becomes clear. The only thing that is done is the elimination of a pseudo-mystery from the domain of science and from the dogma program of[308] pure speculation. The fundamental problem of dualism or of monism remains as fundamental, and as firm[309] as ever.

The metaphysical problem cannot ever be shaken by the discoveries and by the revelations of science……

---

303. ~~of energy,~~ of matter and (of) spirit. ~~These~~
304. human ↑soul
305. be ↑henceforth the
306. sensation /↑sentiment\, such as that of ~~colour~~ fear
307. Friedrich Albert Lange (1828–1875) was a German neo-Kantian philosopher, psychologist, and political theorist. He is known to have developed throughout his works the notion of a "psychology without soul," based on a critique of phrenology and the psychological sciences of his time.
308. the ~~high kingdom~~ ↑dogma program of
309. as ~~a~~ firm

I. III · UNSIGNED

$[15^I$ - 36 a 37$]$

Again, the idea of responsibility is much more extensive than may be thought at first. Popular opinion involves in its sterile ignominy, not only [the] criminal, but his wife also, and his children. It involves at times the place to which he belongs, and even a whole nation is looked upon with disfavour because of the crime of one man.

This consideration may, after a first reading, seem ludicrous, as understanding by responsibility[310] what cannot be included under that name. But a second perusal will manifest its truth to the reader. In what does the primitive movement of imputability consist? In the tracing of an act to the power that produced it. And whither [36^v] is this individual traced? To his family. His family is traced to their home, & from the home ignominy fall upon the district in which that home stands.

Since we are dealing with popular concepts and ideas in this matter, it is well to make a list of all. We shall examine then the common ideas of chance, of law, of free-will, of determinism, of fatalism, of heredity and of responsibility.

We must also examine and consider why false ideas appear at all, and by what defects of reasoning they are produced.

1st. Ignorance of cause.

---

310. by ~~impossib~~ responsibility

[37ʳ]

First of all there is in[311] us a general condition of mind or rather of character by which we pass quickly or slowly from feeling into action.[312] This tendency or general condition has the distinguishing name of impulse. A man is either impulsive or reflexive or normal. When a man is normal there is no tendency behind his faculties to push them to action or to hold them back. His "temptations," his "cravings," his victories of will and his defeats are merely the product of a struggle between the faculties. It [is] as if there were [37ᵛ] no impulse and no reflex at all. (Is this theory true or is it not entirely false?).

In the second place there are[313] the faculties & qualities forming the character, properly[314] speaking, of the man.

In the third place there is the living of the impulse in the faculties, the comparative impulsiveness of the faculties; in simpler language, the force and the weight of the faculties, their development in relation to each other.

[15⁴ – 69]

Conciliation of Being Theory with Cratic Theory.[315]

---

311. is ~~an~~ in
312. /(into action)\ from feeling into action
313. there ~~is~~ are
314. ~~and~~ properly
315. Cratic refers to theories of entropy. Cratic entropy is part of the entropy calculated by the binding process.

Responsibility is an illusion anterior to that of free-will. Responsibility[316] is merely knowing ourselves as Cause. It does not matter that we are determined & therefore, □

We know ourselves merely as a Cause. Responsibility is free from emotional or ethical considerations. Responsibility[317] is often the sense of being, not a cause of wrong, but a cause of unlawfulness.

Acts are the plural manifestations of the universal[318] power by the occasion of the individual character.

[69ᵛ]

Shakespeare's better handling of tragic and tragic-comic[319] (Claudio in "Much Ado") because we realise pain and suffering more deeply than myth.

The individual is (more) moral than the state, society. Society is a curse. The man hates war, prostitution, the citizen loves them, cultivates them. The right to disobey, to rebel. The individual loves modesty *in his family*; the *citizen* detests it, loves vice. Thus the social body, prostitutes. The many suffer that the few may find happiness.

Shoemaker = Boot.

---

316. Resp[onsibility]
317. Resp[onsibility] *is* /↑ ᵐᵃʸ ᵇᵉ\ free from emotional or ethical considerations. Resp[onsibility]
318. univ[ersal]
319. ↑ ᵗʳᵃᵍⁱᶜ⁻comic

[55B – 101]

Responsibility is not moral but purely social; there is no one morally responsible.

Differences[320] between individual and social ethics.

The aim of all social ethics is evident. The 1ˢᵗ thing about social ethics is that it is an ethics of a society. Being [an] ethics of a society, its nature must follow from the nature of society, from the application to society of the principles of general ethics.

What are the principles of general ethics?

Is [an] ethics of necessity social? Every man that is born has a right to live.[321]

Now what is the abstract characteristic of these precepts? That since the end of being born is to live, that[322] which is born should live, and that since the end of being is (rationally) being without pain, that which lives shall live without pain.

[101ᵛ]

Hence we deduce 2 notions: that of end, that of □

|Neither theft nor adultery are crimes, neither [do] they give pain to someone.| crimes against property.[323]

---

320. Diff[eren]ces
321. live. → etc. ↓ pain
322. ~~men~~ that
323. ↑ neither they give pain to someone. → crimes against property

The first rule is all against murder (though painless); the 2ⁿᵈ all against other crimes (that involve pain) small or 1ˢᵗ.

Static and Dynamic Ethics as also of evolution:[324]

(3) that which develops has a right to reach the utmost of its development. I.e., by the 3 rules, each thing has[325] a right to attain its □, its best, and its worst.

quality, quantity.

To each thing its due.

Each thing has a value □

The 1ˢᵗ is a rule of □, the 2ⁿᵈ of goodness, the 3ʳᵈ of beauty.

Interest [in] moral and aesthetic values.

Therefore[326] a person must *mean* value, inspire value? Uplift moral.

[144J-4]

Responsibility is not moral but social. No man is responsible as [an] individual but all [are] responsible[327] as members of a society.

Without determinism there can be no benevolence. For if I think that a man who has done ill has done it

---

324. ↓ as also of evolution:
325. thing ~~must~~ has
326. ∴ [Therefore] a
327. resp[onsibl]e as individual but all resp[onsibl]e

because[328] he chose to do so, having it as completely in his power to do good, obviously I must punish that man pitilessly and justly. But when[329] I perceive that that man is determined in his acts that he is not *responsible* for them, then he can be anything[,] he is led so that ☐

The origin of pity is characteristic and significant. Man began by[330] pitying others — and still humanity is generally so-far [against] physical tortures. And why? Because they recognize men as not responsible[331] for these. In proportion as they think them "responsible" pity |*warns|; there is pity for the hereditary syphilite, but almost none for the one who has acquired syphilis, and if in the latter case there be pity (normally) it is because[332] it is seen, or rather, judged, that the punishment is too great for the fault. Those observations are too obvious to need prolonging or amplifying.

Then comes the carrying of pity [4ᵛ] to the mental domain. The idiot, the madman begins to be pitied. Why? Because they are held to be *not-responsible* for that[333] in which they are deficient or unfortunate.

The sentiment of pity more fundamentally[334] has origin in the sentiment of being injured (any one being

---

328. ∴ [because]
329. when /↑ if \
330. ~~We~~ ↑ Man beg[i|a]n by
331. ~~were~~ recognize men as not ~~ir~~responsible
332. ∴ [because]
333. *not-resp[onsibl]e* for ~~wha~~ that
334. pity ↑ more fundamentally

injured). The little only is pitied when a higher one has struck, even if the punishment be somewhat proportional to a fault of his, he is generally pitied because he is weaker and therefore[335] in a sense injured.

|*Combativeness| and |*non-combativeness| † has the same origin in the self.[336]

Objective classifications made according [to] a process are Subjective, Objective or Subjective-Objective.[337]

Subjective classifications as processes are of exaltation[338] of degrees and of degree-exaltation.

Subject-Object classification[339] according [to] a process are □

---

335. ∴ [because] he is weaker and ∴ [therefore]
336. |*non-c[ombativeness]| † has the same origin. ↓ in the self.
337. sub[jectiv]e, Obj[ectiv]e or Subj[ective]-Obj[ectiv]e
338. Subj[ective] classif[ications] as processes one of exalt[ati]on
339. S[ubject]-Obj[ect] classification

IV – Essay on the Idea of Cause

[15⁴ – 99 a 100]

[100ʳ]³⁴⁰

1.

*Alexander Search*³⁴¹

ESSAY ON THE IDEA OF CAUSE. (EXTRACT).

Schopenhauer has divided the idea of Cause into 3 other ideas properly speaking: Causation, excitation,³⁴² and motivation. The first occurs in the domain of inorganic things; it is characterized³⁴³ by its conformity to the first and to the second laws of Newton. The anterior modification corresponds always to the posterior modification; and action and reaction are equal. Excitation differs from causation in that there is no regular correspondence between the cause and the effect. Motivation is, according to Schopenhauer, causation acting through an intellect. Thus motivation has the character of finality. Every act³⁴⁴ has an end.

---

340. *In the Pessoa Archive the references 15⁴ – 99ʳ e 99ᵛ are catalogued before the references 100ʳ e 100.ᵛ This seems to be an error for the latter references are logically and argumentatively prior to the former.*
341. A[lexander] S[earch]
342. ~~motivation~~ excitation
343. c[h]aracterized
344. ~~hum~~ ↑ᵃᶜᵗ.

Let us examine closely these ideas and see how true they are and how far they go. In the first place it is quite true that causation in the inorganic, inanimate world is[345] rigorously subject to law. Nay more, inanimate[346] things are exempt, as far as we can see, from the law of differences, or, as Leibnitz calls it, the Law of indiscernibles. We are bound to admit that the same amount of heat applied at several times to the same bar of iron will produce in all cases a similar expansion. But □

We are quite justified in saying that *if* the same amount of heat could be trice[347] applied [100ᵛ] to the same bar of iron, it would at all times most[348] certainly produce the same expansion. But, as far as we know, the same fact is not repeated exactly as it was, nor are there, we believe, two like things in the whole universe. The bar of iron we have used is not the bar of iron we use now, third other time. Its radio-activity is indeed infinitesimal; nevertheless it exists and an experiment cannot be the same. The bar of iron is the same and it is not the same. "Being is nothing," said Heraclitus, "and[349] becoming is all."

(Certitude is mathematical and no more. There is no stability in physical things. I cannot divide a thing in half, I must make some mistake. No 2 things in the

---

345. world, is
346. the inanimate
347. trice /↑ several times\
348. would ↑ at all times most
349. for ↑ and

world being equal, it is clear that I cannot divide a thing correctly, that those two empirical halves cannot be equal. But mathematically all this is possible and true. It is true that 4 is the half of 8 and that one[350] half 4 is always equal to the other half 4.)[351]

[99ʳ]

In the first place then we have to make this objection: what Schopenhauer calls causation has nothing at all of cause. The transmission of heat to a bar of iron which results in the partition[352] of the iron molecules, is no relation of cause to effect. It is nothing but a transmission of movement; nothing different from a billiard ball[353] which hits another and stops, imparting to the other its movement. Again if at two different[354] times I throw a stone with equal force[355] — a pure hypothesis, of course — though in different[356] directions, once against a tree, at another time along a clear field,[357] it is obvious that even here there is no question of causation. However diverse[358]

---

350. and ↑ that one
351. half 4.[)]
352. apartition, *in the original. A likely authorial error.*
353. balls
354. diff[eren]t
355. force I
356. diff[eren]t
357. f clear field
358. diff diverse

the movement of the two stones, their movement,[359] in regard to its quantity, is rigorously equal; it cannot but be so, being in both cases the product of an equal force. And a movement must perforce be the product and the continuation of another movement and this one the result of another and thus are linked all the forces and motions of the universe. The so-called causation is nothing but the change from one movement to another, or from one form of movement to another form, or a change of media in the same movement.

[99ᵛ]

Example of football field.[360]

Consider now the form of Cause which Schopenhauer[361] calls excitation. Here we have no longer a movement, for a movement would transmit itself equally. Yet it produces always □

In me and in the man excitation[362] has produced a different effect. It cannot then be a movement; it cannot be conceived as one. Let us consider excitation more closely than we have done. The nature of excitation is,

---

359. movem[en]t
360. *See 173 for the example.*
361. Schop[enhauer]
362. |man| /↑player\ ~~movement~~ excitation

it is said, that there is no real proportion[363] between cause and effect (so to call them) or, better, between the anterior and the consequent modification.

---

363. no ↑real proportion

V – On Error

[15⁵ – 28]

On Error

We shall examine the question of truth, of error, fundamental in philosophy[,] & with it the problem of reality and of appearance, correlated.³⁶⁴

"All roads lead to knowledge," says the problem. "Any road." Here Truth³⁶⁵ excluded, the simple |*extra-philosophical| end, "will lead by □ around." Even so every³⁶⁶ problem[,] implicitly all problems, every philosophical question bases³⁶⁷ directly, if drawn out, in all philosophical questions. The man who gives an opinion is a philosopher at men, save that he ignores³⁶⁸ it. All problems are bound together, as links of a chain, you cannot take one without taking³⁶⁹ the others (|*many find the chain| at the end). Desires of labour, success, particularly³⁷⁰ works of philosophers are mere creations of

---

364. correlated. ~~Not~~
365. T[ruth]
366. ~~the com~~ every
367. ~~is~~ bases
368. ~~ig~~ he ignores
369. take ~~the~~ one without ‡ taking
370. ‡ particularly

mental inventions, cleverness, I may say; every man is a metaphysician and every thought metaphysical.

In hope to push the inquiry into the highest philosophy, drag it into □. To[371] push at the chain, as I have said, till it is finally found and yields no more.

We shall ignore — at |*will| or leave unread — what has little to have with the question and to sound the sea till thy sound stills and goes so further.[372]

[28ᵛ]

"But," you may object, "you argue from a false, or, at least, from a doubtful standpoint." You say the world is a thing conceived, how do I know it?" Simple, I answer, the[373] world is the external result of our complex and compounded sensations.

Take the case of a man thinking himself a genius and not being one. What conclusion[374] is drawn? That man may be in error as to this character.

At least we arrive at the conclusion[375] that error is only impossible in regard to sensation.

---

371. into ~~th~~ □. To
372. ↑ We shall ignore, at |*will| or leave unread – what has little to have with the question. ↓ and to sound the sea till thy sound stills and goes so further.
373. ~~because~~ the
374. conc[lusion]
375. concl[usion]

Hence (1) Body consists in Consciousness;
 (2) Character[376] & personality are objects.

Hence then the fundamental duality is consciousness and not-consciousness.[377] This we find to consist not in matter but in whatever is, as character, as personality, multiple or compound. But multiple and compound is error. Therefore |*Body| consists in consciousness,[378] again we find this.

Here also falseness of theory of immortality of soul, for *multiplicity* of souls is *error*.[379]

[25 – 88][380]
On Error

Error is in sensation and only[381] in sensation. All error proceeds from ignorance (and from haste).

---

376. ~~The~~ Character
377. ~~matter~~ ↑ not consciousness
378. ∴ [Therefore] B[ody] consists in consciouness
379. of imm[ortality] of soul, for *multiplicity* of souls is ~~a~~ error
380. 1. Essay on Sensation.
    2. Essay on Evil.
    3. Essay on Ethics without God.
    4. Essay on Matter and on Motion.
    5. On Parmenides.

    Hachette: Catalogue of Latin authors.

    ~~*Hachette*: On Parmenides "Parmenides."~~
381. ~~not~~ only

For suppose a reasoning from something. This reasoning, suppose, is false. Another reasoning is true. What is the difference between these two acts of reasoning? What is wrong? Is it the reasoning, the mechanism thereof? [88ᵛ] Obviously not, for since one reasoning is true and another is false, and, more, since the mechanism of reasoning cannot be different in one case and in the other, error cannot be in reasoning. It must therefore be in sensation, that is to say, in the way of interpreting a fact by sensation. It follows from this that if we could be absolutely certain that our sensation corresponds to the reality, we could not reason falsely nor fall into error.

(On Error. A commentary on the *Theætetus* of Plato.)

How do we notice error? How do we correct it? How can we tell what is reality?

[25 – 87]

When you say that a thing is bad you use a criterion of good.

Argument from error. If matter be truth it is impossible to err, sensation cannot lead us wrong. (Now error[382] either comes from sensation proper or from reasoning. Both of these, according to the materialists are natural. The principle of error cannot then be in either of them.)[383]

---

382. le[d|a]d us wrong. (Now ~~all~~ error
383. of them.[)]

I. V · UNSIGNED

Error supposes two things, two principles — one fallible, the other infallible. It supposes an infallible principle because it were not *error* unless there were a *truth* to which it might be opposed. It supposes for its existence a principle to which fallibility can be attributed. It supposes, in short, a principle[384] of possibility and a principle of existence.

[87ᵛ]

Thought naturally accompanied languages.

[25 – 89ʳ]

Argument from consciousness bad.

Evil and error of the same nature. The progress of the world towards consciousness is a progress towards evil, towards suffering. There is no consciousness but of imperfections.

Real knowledge identity of idea and thing. So all human knowledge. For me that is true which I make true. For thee that which thou makest true.

The division subject-object in consciousness (most rudimentary thing of all).[385] Limitation, exclusion.

---

384. It supposes ↑, in short, a principle
385. all[)].

VI – On Sensation

[15² – 44]

On Sensation [386]

Sensation has 4 conditions of which 2 are subjective and 2 objective.[387]

The subjective, a priori conditions are:
1. a thing by which there is sensation (subject).[388]
2. a thing of which there is sensation (object).

The objective conditions are:[389]

(1) a brain and a nervous system.
(2) no knowledge by consciousness of that mental operation.

A priori it is clear that in sensation there must be a thing which feels and a thing felt.

---

386. ~~Charada~~
 ← παιδεύω
 παιδεύεις
 παιδεύει
 παιδέυομεν
 παιδέυετε
 παιδέυουσι
 παιδεύετον
 παιδεύετον.

 On Sensation.
387. ~~3~~ 4 conditions of which 2 are subjective and ~~1~~ 2 objective
388. thing ~~conscious~~ ↑ by which there is ↓ sensation ↓ (subject)
389. conditions are ↑ ~~is~~

A posteriori, by science, we ascertain that sensation[390] is always conditioned by a nervous system & by a brain.

[44ᵛ]

These are 4[391] elements which we have for the solution of the problem. Assumedly, having these, we shall be able to arrive at some conclusion.[392]

[15B¹ – 70]

———

Let us endeavour to see what are the data of the study of sensation.

We notice then:
(1) Every phenomenon of sensation is conditioned by a brain, by a[393] nervous system, by a body in fine.
(2) These conditions are ignored by consciousness. "*La conscience est nullement anatomiste.*" (Binet)[394]

---

390. that ~~science~~ sensation
391. [3|4]
392. conclusion.
    → De †
393. ↑ᵇʸ a
394. Alfred Binet (1857–1911) was a French psychologist and the inventor of the intelligence texts that are the basis of the commonly known I.Q. test. He wrote a book entitled *L'âme et le corps*, which discusses the primordial role of sensation in the constitution of knowledge. Pessoa's reading notes on this book are in the Pessoa Archive [BNP/E3, 15⁵ – 81: "Notes on *L'âme et le corps*"].

(3) Every consciousness is in a subject and of an object. This is the famous relation subject-object, which is denied by M. Binet, because, as he says, "*le sujet ne serait qu'un objet déguisé.*" But I see no reason to deny it.

[70ᵛ]

There are, therefore, these things to be explained:
(1) How an "external" object (an "*x de la matière*") can transmit its own image along the nerves to centres of vision in the brain.
(2) How a consciousness is not of the movement of molecules which gives the sensation.[395]
(3) □

Let us suppose, in the first place, that there is properly speaking no organ of vision, no eye, and that we fake consciousness of this movement[396] of molecules, by *feeling* their motion, and that this consciousness of resistance *is* the sensation of vision.

Or we may say that we have no consciousness of this movement[397] of molecules, because this is *the material side* of the sensation of vision. Everything mental has something material which[398] manifests it and represents it.

---

395. How ↑ there is no ↓ ᵃ consciousness is not of the mov[emen]t and of molecules which gives her her ↑ the sensation
396. mov[emen]t
397. mov[emen]t
398. spirit mental is has something material keep which

[15B² – 28 a 31]
Essay on Sensation

The "external"[399] object is either analogous to the sensation or not. If analogous it is the sensation itself.

If not then we perceive only something of the object and there is consequently a *noumenon*. I do not see how a[400] sensation can reproduce exactly, give an exact idea of an external object; how a thing felt in the mind can[401] be an exact reproduction of something other than mental. Bergson.

[29ʳ]

1st. *Conclusion.* We know no more than our sensations.

After this we can consider sensation either in itself (philosophic method), or in a relation[402] (scientific method).

Considering sensation in itself, the inevitable conclusion is that its conditions are [at] the turn concepts of time and of space. A sensation must have a duration and it must take place somewhere (and be the effect of some movement).

Considering sensation in a sense purely[403] scientific, we must argue, as does M. Binet, that sensation sup-

---

399. ~~Sensation is ei~~ The "external"
400. how ~~the~~ a
401. felt ↑in the mind can
402. in ↑a relation
403. a ↑sense purely

poses a brain, a nervous system, and these presuppose extension and duration, space and time, and so on to the establishing of all empirical notions.

The first consideration is obviously correct: sensation, however we consider it needs space and time; but the argument is not so absolutely self-tenable, axiomatic that sensation presupposes a nervous system because this is a[404] gratuitous assumption on the transcendental, true reality of the visible universe.

[30ʳ]
On Sensation

If all things be sensation, then the nervous system is also a sensation. And if it be so, then it is not an intermediary between us and the "external object." But it does not follow, as M. Binet thinks, that therefore[405] we see things just as they are. What follows is that sensation cannot be explained by us[406] from the nervous system. Sensation has to be considered in itself. To say sensation[407] depends on the nervous system is to say sensation itself depends on something it produces, for the nervous system is a sensation, and no more.

The nervous system is something which occupies space, etc., a sensation of ours also.

---

404. presupposes ↑ᵃ nervous system because this is /↑ᵇᵃˢᵉᵈ\ a
405. ∴ [therefore]
406. by ↑ᵘˢ
407. say ~~orig~~ sensation

[30ᵛ]

Let us then see what is the meaning of, and the explanation for, the nervous system.

I localise in space, and as a thing having extension, the chain which is in this room two or three yards away. Now it is desirous that in localizing such a thing as a chain by sensation it would be extremely ridiculous, ludicrous were I not to localize myself, were I to conceive a thing as in space and myself as out of it. No; localizing anything, I must localize myself.

By being thus ideated a thing with a nervous system I become the possibility of many sensations.

[31ʳ]

Atoms are, must be conceived as all alike. (?) In them there is plurality pure. It is only in complex formations that plurality becomes differentiation. Yet the atoms must be mere concepts, since nothing existent is like any other thing.

1 atom oxygen & 2 atoms hydrogen and the same again make the same quantity[408] of water — 1 molecule; yet these 2 compounds must be different[409] though they contain like and equal, elements. Difference[410]

---

408. ~~volume~~, quantity
409. diff[eren]t
410. Diff[eren]ce

begins in the molecules. (Or are atoms infinitesimally different?)[411]

1st Law of thought: Negativity.
Absolute things have a singular negativity.
Relative things a *plural* negativity.
E.G., 0 and ∞
12 and all other numbers.

2nd Law. Principle of Identity. If a thing had no negative, it would be idle, useless to say it is[412] itself, since it can be nothing else.

[31ᵛ]
Essay on Sensation

☐

[15B³- 59]

1. The nervous system, the brain cannot[413] explain sensation, because the brain and the nervous system are themselves things of sensation. The sensation of colours cannot be properly explained by a movement, because both colour and movement[414] are sensations. (?)

(Movement[415] may be anterior to colour in evolution)

---

411. diff[eren]t
412. ~~was~~ ↑ is
413. ↑, the brain cannot
414. mov[emen]t
415. Mov[emen]t

Consciousness is the only immaterial thing that exists, not human consciousness, but general conscience,[416] atomic consciousness, I believe.[417]

[59ᵛ]

Chapter of sensation, in the relations of matter and of spirit.

---

1. Sensation is conditioned by a nervous system.
2. Consciousness ignores a nervous system; it has no consciousness of the inter-cerebral movement.

Theories:

a) The inter-cerebral movement[418] is the representation of the sensation.
b) It *is* the sensation. It is by the inter-cerebral movement,[419] observed, that we know a man has sensation. It is the *scientific* side of the sensation □

---

416. general ↑ conscience
417. I believe.

Essay on Free-Will to begin by a consideration of matter and of spirit.

Nature of the science of Ontology.
Science treats of Laws, (of multiple things), ontology does not.

418. The inter-c[erebral] mov[emen]t
419. mov[emen]t

$[15B^3 - 99^r]$

The higher the human type, the less acute the physical senses, with the exception of TOUCH (or rather "sensibility").

Is sensibility [420] the physical expression of an inner personality.

$[15B^4 - 77a \text{ a } 77]$[421]

$[77^r]$
Consciousness

I have not consciousness of my body, nor sensation of it; I am conscious of my sensations.

All is sensation. All what we call the external world is a sensation and no more.

I have *consciousness* [422] of an arm which has been cut off. This is *incomplete* sensation, my sensation of sight, touch, are not in accord with this.

I sleep — my brain is there; wherefore am I not conscious of my body?

---

420. ~~the~~ sensibility
421. $[15B^4 - 77a]$
  ~~The Theories of Science.~~
  ~~Spinozism,~~ pantheism.
  ~~Space before Science.~~
  ~~Space. Time~~
422. *consciousness* /↑ sensation\

VII – Essay on Heraclitus

[15¹ – 52 a 54]

Essay on Heraclitus [423]

Heraclitus

We know 2 things by experience: one, that we have of the "exterior" world an image fundamentally immutable, that such "exterior" world yields our laws and invariabilities; second, that all in nature is in perpetual motion. Now, how is it possible to have any knowledge of the universe [424] if all is in perpetual motion and every thing is ceaselessly [425] becoming another?

The hypotheses are 4:
Subject and object both immutable.
Subject and object both in motion.
Subject immutable and object in motion.
Subject in motion and object immutable. [426]
Let us see what kind of a world this gives us.

---

423. Ess[ay] on He[raclitus]
424. ~~ext~~ universe
425. ~~in~~ ceaselessly
426. Subj[ect] and obj[ect] both immutable
Subj[ect] and obj[ect] both in motion
Subj[ect] immutable and obj[ect] in motion
subj[ect] in motion and obj[ect] immutable.

If subject and object are both immutable, truth is immediate. No search of truth is needed. To search is to move, to inquire is to think, to think is to be altered.

Besides experience[427] contradicts this for immutability before immutability cannot yield anywhere motion.

[52ᵛ]

(2) The second case: motion of both □
(3) The 3ʳᵈ case Object in motion and subject[428] immutable renders all perception impossible — it is the interpretation Plato puts upon the system of Heraclitus.
(4) If Object is in and Subject[429] is in motion, really then □

Let us see the data of experience:[430] it gives us motion as reality and immutability[431] as appearance. What can produce this. Not (1) for (reasons above) nor (4) because in these matter is[432] considered immutable. (3) and (2) remain. Now (3) cannot explain, for □

(2) is left as where Subject and Object move *in the same way* Subject takes knowledge of the object as immutable.[433]

---

427. exp[erience]
428. Obj[ect] in motion and subj[ect]
429. Obj[ect] is in and Subj[ect]
430. exp[erience]:
431. immut[ability]
432. ~~not~~ ↑ⁿᵒʳ ([2|4]) ∴ ~~perception is only appearance~~ ↑ᵇᵉᶜᵃᵘˢᵉ ⁱⁿ ᵗʰᵉˢᵉ ᵐᵃᵗᵗᵉʳ is
433. ~~rem~~ ↑ⁱˢ left as where S[ubject] and O[bject] move *in the same way* S[ubject] takes knowledge of the o[bject] as immutable.

Before perception all things are immutable; this is because Subject & Object move together,[434] are the same.

But before Reason (Science) the Universe is in motion.
Apply again 4 arguments.

What can give |*them| all motion? It's an immutable before an ever-changing Object or its eternal change before an object[435] which is immutable.

[53ʳ]

Power and Act are 2 successive states of anything in the world.

Heraclitus

πῦρ[436] ἀεί ζῶον = a fire always living.

Suppose a thought which should think itself. It cannot think itself as itself, for that would not be thought. It thinks as[437] consciousness; it thinks itself as a primitive matter, as a kind of æther, as the[438] πῦρ ἀεὶ ζῶον of Heraclitus. Indeed the expression "fire always living"

---

434. ↑S[ubject] and O[bject] move together
435. Obj[ect] or its eternal change before an obj[ect]
436. ̶π̶ πῦρ
437. i̶t̶ as
438. ↑ᵃˢ the

is good;[439] it gives the idea of an "appearance which thinks." But this primitive matter *is* thought; this matter is an act a pure act. Now thought, force, (En) [53ᵛ] is pure[440] power.

But pure Power = pure Act for pure Power is *complete* Power and is therefore acting power, that is pure *act*.[441]

The Universe is a "thought which exists." It is a tangible form of thought.

Hurting the representation you hurt the thing represented.

Ways into the problem:
1. Critique of sensation
2. Cause (?)

In the spiritual world, even, there must be law, according[442] to Dr. □ (see his critique of Bushnell who had said that the apparent[443] world was "incommunicably separate from ours"). Then there is no free-will, all being determined. (Law is the principle of determination).

---

439. ~~the best~~ ↑good
440. ~~that~~ pure
441. ↑pure *act*
442. acc[ording]
443. ap[parent]

[54ʳ]

The external universe cannot be infinite.

    For the infinite is indetermined, & therefore[444] unreal.

    An infinite world is [445] an indetermined determination.

Subjective argument: the world is infinite, because it has no ideal end. Thought finds no end to the universe; that is, the universe[446] has no rational end; that is, no ideal end.

    If the materialist still contends that the universe[447] is infinite, he must allow that the rational is the real. Now follow Hegel.

    Objective argument: by atoms.

[22 – 42]

Il y a de l'être dans toute proposition (Leibniz).

On Heraclitus. Universal motion may be very slow and so sensation be possible.[448] (Radio-activity).

---

444. ∴ [therefore]
445. is /↑ would be\
446. univ[erse]
447. mat[eriali]st still contend that the univ[erse]
448. be — possible

Heraclitus says that all is motion. But what is motion? Something which is conceived only as opposed to substance.

Moreover, motion demands two things: a thing that moves and a thing moved, a motor and a mobile. — It needs, 1ˢᵗ, a thing to move because, nothing can unceasingly move itself. It needs, 2ˡʸ, a thing to be moved, for nothing can move itself, as I have said.

[42ᵛ]

Again, to perceive anything, to have any cognition, it is necessary that he that has such a cognition should be something.

That is to say, all motion, all perception, all knowledge, be it changeful and of a thing that changes supposes a substance, if by no fact but than that it *is* here, be it for less than a moment.

Now, having seen that all things are movement, there is one question more to decide. This movement either exists or does not exist. If it do[449] not exist, still as it may be said of it that it exists[,] for it appears to exist[,] the idea[450] of existence is *prior* to the idea of movement and existence cannot consist in motion.

---

449. does

450. ↑ for it appears to exist the idea

$[15^1 - 86^r]$

A vida é a morte. A vida do todo depende da morte de mil cellulas.[451]

Cf. Heraclito

The life of society as[452] the death of individuals, the life of mankind as the death of societies,[453] the life of the universe as the death of the universe, the life of all as the death of all.

$[86^v]$

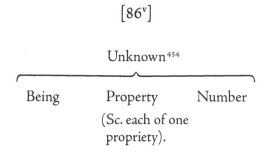

---

451. *Translation*: Life is death. The life of the whole depends on the death of a thousand cellules.
452. of ↑as
453. of its societies
454. Unknown Unknown

ON HERACLITUS

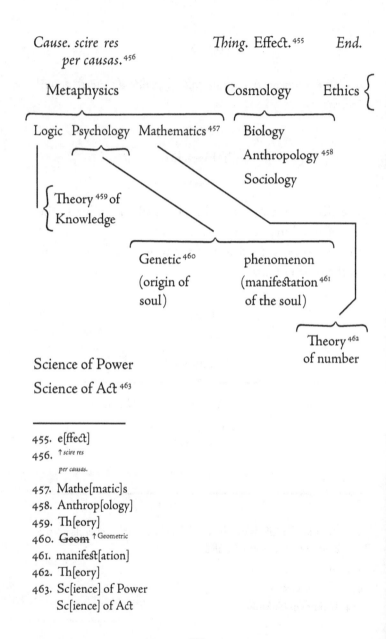

Cause. scire res per causas.[456] *Thing.* Effect.[455] End.

Metaphysics   Cosmology   Ethics {

Logic Psychology Mathematics[457]   Biology
                                      Anthropology[458]
                                      Sociology

{ Theory[459] of Knowledge

Genetic[460]   phenomenon
(origin of   (manifestation[461]
soul)   of the soul)

Theory[462] of number

Science of Power
Science of Act[463]

---

455. e[ffect]
456. ↑ *scire res per causas.*
457. Mathe[matic]s
458. Anthrop[ology]
459. Th[eory]
460. ~~Geom~~ ↑ Geometric
461. manifest[ation]
462. Th[eory]
463. Sc[ience] of Power
     Sc[ience] of Act

I. VII · UNSIGNED

$$[15^5-57]$$

Heraclitus Obscure — [464]
   Cosmology. Psychology. Physical metaphysics.

Life (a mode) (of) radioactivity.
   (*waste*) radiation.

A thing is at the same time living and dead. Life is death. A thing that is living is dying all the while.

Therefore[465] Living is not *Life*, neither is dying *Death*. Life,[466] Living, death: these are the 3 forms of thinking things. That which is Living is in correspondence with an environment. That which is *dead* is out of the correspondence with an environment.[467] (Either is ceaselessly dying to an environment[468] and living to a new one).

Follow the human being from the cytula to his late[469] death (to a death late in life). [57ᵛ] The cytula is produced by the fecundation of the ovum[470] by the spermatozoon. But itself it is neither the egg nor the spermatozoon,

---

464. Heracl[itus] Obscure —
465. ∴ [Therefore]
466. ~~Life~~ Life
467. en[vironmen]t
468. en[vironmen]t
469. his ↑ᵃ late
470. ovum ^(↑ egs)

nor a mere sum of these. It is the form of their production, not that itself. It is a unity. 1 + 2 may make 3 but 3 is neither 1 nor 2 nor the sum of 1 + 2; it is the *form* of that sum. Without the 1 + 2 there were no 3 but the 3 is by itself a number and a form. (The world is caused, says Schopenhauer,[471] by its perpetual (*apopos*) destruction.)[472]

It's not a mechanical mixture that takes place, but that subtler thing called a chemical change.

Same occurs when 2 atoms H meet 1 of oxygen. That which they compose contains really 1 part of one and 2 of the other. But it is neither O nor H: it is water.

[58ʳ]

Death comes. What is death? A failing of correspondence with an environment.

Is the man completely dead? Science says that he is. He has then fallen out of the correspondence with *all* environments?[473] He has then passed[474] entirely to nothing? How can this be? When the body is decomposed, the matter of which it is formed does not die materially. The organism loses correspondence with its environment;[475] but the □

---

471. Schop[enhauer],
472. ↓ ⁽*apopos*⁾ destruction
473. Sc[ience] says that he is. He has then fallen out of the c[orrespondence] with *all* en[vironmen]ts
474. He ↑ ʰᵃˢ ᵗʰᵉⁿ passed
475. corr[espondence] w[ith] its en[vironmen]t

Non minus maior. No man will[476] die *completely.*

A certain form, having reached a certain point[477] passes to nothing! How?

[25 – 69 a 69a]

My first action was to inquire of myself whether man's perpetual failure in the ground of higher thought was due to want of reasoning power, or to an ill use of his reasoning.[478] It appeared strange to me that we should be able to discuss the questions of metaphysics and of psychology with such subtlety and yet be unable to come to any conclusion in these fields that it found not an immediate answer, and hence onward in an infinite progression.

I concluded hastily that one of two hypotheses must be right: either man failed through improper or impersistent application of his intellect, or failed by the want of primary critique of reason.

[69ᵛ]

Popular opinion admits a God; true, but it is but the idea of God, which persists in all men, clothed in the accidents (so to speak) of theology. In India, the idea of God

---

476. ↑ᴺᵒ ᵐᵃⁿ ʷⁱˡˡ shall not
477. p[oin]t
478. of ~~the~~ ↑ʰⁱˢ reasoning

is other; the instinct is the same. Among the negroes the idea is other;[479] the instinct is the same. It is the intellect that diversely clothes the same body.

Critique Critique
CRITIQUE OF THE THEORY OF HERACLITUS:

All is change. True. But if there is but change, this change must take place *in something*. This something is what we call substance, Being.

Any 2 opposite opinions are absolutely identical.
All that begins has a cause (Vallet).[480]
It was very soon clear to me that antinomies must have some explanation. I found the contrast of 2 opinions a false contrast. To conciliate two things, it is needful [69a] that they should be of the same nature. I can contrast an apple and a pear, but not an apple and a cat. And the fact of these theories being antithetic I found to be the fact that they were of a different[481] nature, one being a priori, the other being deduced from experience.

(Examination of Zeno's Achilles and turtle paradox, as contrasted with a normal argument pro movement).

---

479. ab other
480. In Charles Robert Anon's reading diary, a 1906 entry refers to Pierre Vallet's *Histoire de la Philosophie*. The second chapter of this book is dedicated to Greek philosophy and was one of the sources for the discussion of Heraclitus' thought.
481. dif[feren]t

[133 – 8]

I often think that it is not thoughts which are too deep for tears, but tears which are too deep for thought.
Alexander Search [482]

[8ᵛ]

πάντων πραγμάτων μέτρον ἄνθρωπος
Man is the measure of all things.

πολεμὸς ματὴρ πάντων

ἩΡΑΚΛΕΙΤΟΣ
πῦρ ἀεί ζῶον
fire always living.

Theory of the Soul — *Simile of Smoke*.
Suppose that the only primitive thing the only thing that exists and that □

---

482. A[lexander] S[earch]

VIII – On Thomas Aquinas

[15¹ – 26 a 27]

Thomas Aquinas' theory of "physical premotion" is indeed admirable & new. At first sight it seems easy to refute; no sooner, however, do we ponder it in its real meaning and essence than we are, first, astonished at its strength, secondly, after being convinced of its inaccuracy, of the difficulty of its refutation.

Nevertheless it can be refuted.

Thomas Aquinas[483] says that God determines all things that act; he determines one to be determined in the action[484] and he determines others to be free. Thus, in this last point, there is a conciliation of divine power and the freedom of the human will.

The theory appears[485] easy to refute at first because[486] it seems to be evident that since God determines this and that, all things are determined. But soon we understand all the subtlety (we do not mean |*distinct| subtlety) of the idea. It is true that all things determined are determined; but those[487] things determined to be free, absolutely are, of their own nature, free, by that very

---

483. T̶h̶ Thomas ↑Aquinas
484. determined ↑in the action
485. s̶e̶e̶m̶s̶ ↑appears
486. ∴ [because]
487. a̶l̶l̶ those

determination. God, Thomas argues or means to argue, creates not only things [26ᵛ] but also, of course, *the natures* of things; therefore if he creates a thing determined, it is determined; and if he creates a thing free, it is free.⁴⁸⁸ This argument, as far as it goes, is invulnerable.

It is as if a despot gives this command: "when I command *disobey me*." This is not probable at all, but it is conceivable. It is not probable because the nature of a command⁴⁸⁹ is not to order one not to do what is told.

But, for instance, a man will[ing] to fits of insecurity may say to his children: if I command such or such a thing (or not, he might finally bid them [to] do [that] in a fit of these) *do not obey me*. Here is a case, not only conceivable,⁴⁹⁰ but probable. The idea of disobedience is entirely antagonistic to that of command. The father bid his children obey him by disobeying him. This is just the case in St. Thomas' argument: God *determines* men *to be free*.

It may perhaps seem ridiculous or fantastic to make a comparison of this kind;⁴⁹¹ but we ask the reader to consider its aptness and not its extravagant nature. There is [an] exact analogy with the two cases, except of course in the nature of the 2ⁿᵈ (insignificant), which we might have subordinated for another more normal.

---

488. create[s] a thing determined, it is determined; and if he create[s] a thing free, ~~he creates~~ it is free
489. ∵ [because] the nature of ↑ ᵃ command
490. ~~probable~~ ↑ ᶜᵒⁿᶜᵉⁱᵛᵃᵇˡᵉ
491. ~~ph~~ fantastic to make a comparison ~~like this~~ ↑ ᵒᶠ ᵗʰⁱˢ ᵏⁱⁿᵈ

I. VIII · UNSIGNED

We have come now to the stage where we feel ourselves bound to admire the subtle[492] thing of the "Analogy of the Scholars."

[27ʳ]

Now comes the refutation.

When there is such a contradiction as that in the question between the created nature of a thing and the very nature of creation, there must be a motive for it. It must have a purpose.

Aquinas let us enter into the spirit of the theory and see if it be tenable.

"God creates some things determined"— this only is easy to understand; "and some things are free," this is not so easy to understand, but, as we have shown, is not nevertheless incomprehensible. All this can pass. But there is one thing that cannot pass. It is the idea that God has created the *nature* of some things [as] determined and the *nature* of other things [as] *free*. The *nature* of things[493] and the idea of freedom exclude one another. There is no[494] *free nature*. "Determining a thing to be free" we can understand as it is. But "to make freedom[495] the nature of a thing" is not sense.

---

492. a̶c̶o̶u̶n̶t̶ subtle
493. t̶h̶i̶n̶g̶ things
494. n̶o̶t̶ no
495. t̶h̶e̶ freedom

The *nature*[496] *of a thing* implies determination.

So long as we put the phrase in this way: "God determines a thing to be free" we may think we are talking sense; no longer so when we turn[497] the expression to "God makes *the nature* of things *free.*"

[27ᵛ]

Because what is the meaning of the nature of a thing? The fixed principle of its existence as *that* thing and no other. The nature of a thing implies laws of that nature; and freedom means to have no laws. Therefore the expression cannot be said.

Freedom would mean: to have no nature at all. But if we say: "God created things whose nature is to have no nature at all," we are not talking sense or anything[498] like it may mean.

[15²–80]

St. Thomas' a coherent theory that is in which the Secondary theories are true relatively to the basis, which may be false, as it is here.

This world *is* the unknown, save that it is the Unknown[499] as we see it, as we know it.[500]

---

496. ~~ph~~ *nature*
497. ~~for no~~ turn
498. ~~sh~~ anything
499. Unk[nown]
500. know it. /(perceive it).\

Hallucinations. If what we see in[501] this case be not there, our eyes are not to be trusted.

The difference from *things* is only in there being *not-universal perception.* The external world is a *universal hallucination.*

[80ᵛ]

Thus goes the basis of the philosophic system of Thomas, and the[502] foundation of the theories and of the dogmas of the Catholic Church (nay, of all Churches).

On Thomas Aquinas[503]

As it is, it is quite right; all[504] of them are false; there is not one which is conceivable.

Ibidem[505]

I.e., theories, at all points adherent though, of St. Thomas.

Now, how did this arise? It is very simple. One man willed differently from the other;[506] of this there is no question. But why, how,[507] did one will *this* and the other will *that*?

---

501. ~~in~~ in
502. ↑and the
503. *On Th[omas] Aquinas*
504. ~~of~~ all
505. Ibid[em]
506. from /↑to\ the other
507. why, /↑how,\

The 2 wills — the wills of these 2 men — are either determined or indetermined. If they be determined they are not free.

Let us consider the hypothesis of the indeterminate volition, the theory[508] of free-will, which asserts volition to determine itself, i.e., to be indetermined.

Indeterminateness of will = infinity in volition.

---

508. ~~will~~ ↑volition, the ~~hypo~~ ↑theory

IX – Essay on Pascal

[144 T – 43ᵛ a 44]

Essay on Pascal

Influence of Catholic[509] Church on thought (Bad). For me, when it is said of Pascal that he *lusts* by converting to a man, a certain girl, this is more perfect than, and I had rather had it so, that Pascal had lusted [after] her by seeking her. In some of its aspects even [a] prostitute is better than mundane (enclosure is necessary).

That denying of all happiness to mankind is the worst thing that can be done; the worst crime that can be wreaked upon poor humanity.[510]

[44ʳ]

Why that cold hate in the name of God? Why that torture of soul in the name of Christ? The tortures of the Inquisition were[511] bad, horrible, unspeakable, but worse, horribler, more unspeakable[512] the tortures of soul than in Christianity and in all that the Catholic Church has

---

509. Cath[olic]
510. ~~men~~ ↓ humanity
511. ~~are~~ were
512. more unspeakable /↑ less speakable\

wreaked[513] upon the world. And that talk[514] of a state of death being a state of perfection is the worst outrageous nonsense. It is an insult to the intellect.

The history of lust is a history of lust[515] and men. The history of Christianity is a history of *lust & madness*. What man □

[44ᵛ]

I feel a coldness at heart when thinking of those men, cold, womanless, having no love,[516] no □, no wealth,[517] for when a man has a thing to be avoided and a desire a thing to be pent.[518] Ignorance testing itself, external[519] life the ghost not even of success, not that □.

The[520] bad passions that may sin for sexual intercourse are[521] small for those that may sin from the lack of it □.

Examine attentively.

[26 – 84ʳ]

Pascal, you will remember, said that he accepted the Christian religion because it was in such a way contrary

---

513. ~~worked~~ ↑ wreaked
514. ~~of nonsense~~ ↑ talk
515. ~~lust~~ lust
516. ~~desires~~ love
517. no ~~s~~ □, wealth ‡
518. ~~pen~~ pent
519. ~~whereof a~~ external
520. ~~Wh~~ The
521. ₸ are

to all logic. And there is here the gem of a judicious observation. For indeed all religions and all creeds have striven consciously or unconsciously to make the most mad assertions and to talk the most complete nonsense that every man can conceive. And, indeed, it is only by our observing that such nonsense is conceived, and actually here in the middle of us, that we can believe it entered ever into the mind of man.

X – On the Limits of Science

[28 – 99ᵛ]

C. R. Anon

On the Limits of Science

Empirical investigation can lead to nothing, for it is based upon an illusion — on a coherent illusion, but nonetheless on an illusion. When I say can lead to nothing, I mean it cannot be made the basis of a philosophic system.

Idea of immortal life not horrible. It would be horrible if it were immortal life of body & mind together. Immortal life of the soul alone is not horrible but natural and pleasing to it.

PART II.
Addenda

Further Writings concerning Rationalism — I
Preliminary Sketches for the "Essay on the Nature and Meaning of Rationalism"—1.1

1ˢᵗ Stage

[15⁵ – 78 – 79]

[79ʳ]

Essay on the Nature & Meaning of Rationalism

New definition of Rationalism: — Rationalism[522] is that system of investigation which substitutes, in the internal □, □.

Rationalism[523] may be that there is something beyond reason, but since reason is the □ of the internal reality, such a reality is above the[524] internal world, and therefore[525] unreachable, inutile, as if it existed not.

A wrong of faith: — All science (in a sense as wide as can be: search for truth)[526] is the elimination of the personal factor.

---

522. R[ationalism]: — R[ationalism]
523. R[ationalism]
524. reason, in contr the internal
525. ∴ [therefore]
526. ↑: search for truth

It is not that the truth of Religion[527] is particular because[528] it may be □.

The fact that the idea of God is universal — hereof quite true — pure nothing because[529] the idea of God is not a *sensation*, but an *intuition*, i.e., is mental.[530] It has to be subordinated to moral experimentation, i.e., to reason(ing).[531]

[79ᵛ]

Science and the exterior world.

Science and sensation. — Sun seems to move.

Science shows it does not.

Experimentation.[532]

Physics		*Psychology*[533]
Science	=	Reason — □[534]
Experimentation	=	Reasoning — □
Observation		

---

527. Rel[igion]
528. ∵ [because]
529. true – ↑pure nothing ∵ [because]
530. an *intuition* ↑i.e., is mental
531. ~~seeing~~ reason(ing)
532. ~~Relat~~ Experimentation.
533. Psych[ology]
534. ~~in the~~ □

Pure Rationalism[535] — not distinguished from distrusted Rationalisms[536] such as Hæckel's, □.

Rationalism[537] not a system of metaphysics, not a system at all, but a method,[538] a philosophical method.

Philosophy proper[539] is dived into:

(1) Method (Rationalistic science)[540]

(2) Theory of knowledge (Critics)   ? on this one

(3) Theory of Being (Metaphysics)

Science into 3; (1)[541] Method   (1) Abstraction and
                 (2) □   (2) □   Experience[542]
                 (3) Cosmology[543]   (3) □

(Theory of Exterior)

V. S |*Cousin| — The question of Scientific method is not of science but of philosophy.[544]

---

535. R[ationalis]m
536. R[ationalis]ms
537. R[ationalism]
538. R[ationalism] not as systems of metaphysics ↑ not a system at all, but a ~~metaph~~, method
539. *Philosophy* ↑ proper
540. sc[ience]
541. ([2|1])
542. Exp[erience]
543. g Cosmology
544. → V.S/
    |*Cousin| – The question of Sc[ienti]fic method is not of sc[ience] but of philosophy.

[78ʳ]

Rationalism

When you say that all things should be subordinated to reason it occurs to us to ask: *Why?* What is there in reason to give it this right? It must be something in the nature of reason; now this, whatever it is, is perceived either intuitively and that is to say, reason affirms itself immediately as competent- or reflexively,[545] by examining, analyzing the nature of reason. If the first, Rationalism[546] contradicts itself, for this intuition, this immediate *spiritual* or *mental* perception is precisely what it rejects faith and spiritualism[547] for having. If the second, how is Rationalism[548] to analyse reason? With reason of course; but either[549] this is impossible, or, if held possible, reason is held |*proving| its claim immediately and here we are again at the first hypothesis, that of faith, so persistently attacked by Rationalism.[550]

[78ᵛ]

The answer is at hand. What do we seek? Evidence. What is the faculty that □ evidence? Reason, by its very nature, by its very definition. But how do we know it?[551]

---

545. is reflexively
546. R[ationalism]
547. be spiritualism
548. R[ationalism]
549. what either
550. R[ationalis]m
551. ↓ But how do we know it?

But what is evidence.

But the Christian claims that the religious sense is of the nature of a perception. — But it[552] may be an illusion. How do we, in the material universe, test if a perception is an illusion? By comparing it with the universal perception, i.e., the view of the external world common to the most of men, i.e., reality[553] — Analogically how would, in the spiritual, mental world, a hallucination[554] be told? By comparing it with *internal universal perception.*[555] But what is internal universal perception?[556] The answer is easy and conclusive: it is *reason.*

Reality & Reason

Thus rationalism is justified. As intuitions of the sense-world must be subordinated to the sense-world rule: sensation to the universal internal reality; so intuitions[557] of the soul-world must be subordinated to the soul-world rule and reason. Rationality is internal reality.

True, this may be a universal illusion (all may be an illusion) but we can do no harm to Reason.[558]

---

552. it /↑ a perception\
553. men, ↑ i.e., reality
554. we in the spiritual, mental world a halluc[inat]ion. *The word "we" has not been included above since we consider it an authorial lapse.*
555. *internal universal perception* /↑ internal reality reality.\
556. i[nternal] u[niversal] p[erception] /↑ u[niversal] reality\
557. sensation [to the] ↑ univ[ersal] i[nternal] reality; so int[uiti]ons
558. . ← True, this may be a universal illusion (all may be an illusion) but we can do no harm to Reason.

2nd Stage

[15³ – 37 – 45]

Rationalism [559]

It is not easy to pass from rationalism to faith: only the rationalist is a staunch disbeliever. The sceptic easily falls into faith, because scepticism is tiresome and, besides, does not exist.[560] The atheist is a believer & does not [561] change his belief when he becomes a Catholic[562] — for it is generally the opposite, and equally extreme, form of belief that he |chooses| to |*inculcate| to. But the rationalist, accustomed by temperament to admit everything in the things outside reason, and to have maybe as the matter of his darkness, does not easily lapse into the contrary of himself. He is already his own contrary. He is a substantially an acceptor or admitter, a sightseer of theories and of speculations.[563]

[38ʳ]

Rationalism

Rationalism enables us to enjoy all moods because every mood is a possibility of truth.

---

559. Rat[ionalis]m
560. tiresome ↑ and, besides, does not exist.
561. ~~can~~ ↑ does not
562. a Catholic ↑ another believe
563. contrary. ↑ He is a substantially ← an acceptor or admitter, a right seer of theories and ↑ of speculations.

If a man say(s) that the Sun wheels round the earth, I cannot accept his creed. If he says that the whole world wheels round God, I have no objection to admitting it.

If a man says that he saw a □ in the street □, I deny his statement and presume he was drunk; if a man says he saw a † in this street, I may doubt but I have no valid argument just against his testimony. I have no evidence that † do not exist and may not therefore exist in any street.[564]

[38ᵛ]

If a man says a miracle occurred and a lame man has suddenly got one of his legs, I easy allow the fact, after testing it, and leave the miracle, which is an |*artefact|, as an apparent question for metaphysics.

[39ʳ]
Rationalism

Rationalists are generally conservatives and aesthetes.
There is no humanism outside Rationalism.

[40ʳ]
Rationalism [565]

Rationalism is expressedly rare & tendentially common. The literature of thought (apart from Greece) contains

---

564. exist ← and ~~therefore~~ may not therefore exist in every street.
565. Rat[ionalis]m

few expressions of rationalism. If [566] we consider that Kant is the typical rationalist, and how few thinkers resemble Kant, we will understand this. Yet the man in the street [567] is often a rationalist in his instinctive way; the common phrase about a superstition, [568] "there may be something in it," is an exact expression of the rationalistic attitude.

[41ʳ]
Rationalism [569]

Kant's creation not only of the distinction between the subject and the object [570] and between *noumenon* and *phainomenon*, but also of one of [571] the main distinctions of rationalism — the one between pure and practical reason.

───

Rationalists have, in politics, a conservative indifferentism. Political life respects them concerning to its irrationality and the paradox [572] of having to act without any scientific guidance.

───

566. ↑ The [L|l]iterature of thought ↑ (apart from Greece) contains few expressions of rationalism. But If
567. the /↑ any\ street
568. a ↑ some superstition ↑ or another
569. Rat[ionalis]m
570. Kant's creation ↑ not only of the distinction between subject /↓ the subjective\ and object /↓ the objective\
571. of ↑ one of
572. irr irrationality and the impossibility of paradox

Rationalism tends to aestheticism, if it does not positively generate it.

A devout Catholic will hardly enjoy [573] a brilliant satire on the Pope. A rationalist will enjoy even a scurrilous felicity on rationalism; for it is one of the principles of rationalism to admit the possibility of being wrong. [574]

[43ʳ] [575]
Rationalism [576]

Infinity and eternity cannot be predicted of any material or real thing, because reality is concrete and infinite [577] and eternity abstract; to say space is infinite is to say space does not exist; to say time lasts eternally is to say time does not last, but is a fair abstract "point."

If space be limited, there is no "beyond" it or "outside" it.

If *space* be limited, outside and beyond it there is not-space.

---

573. ↑ proudly enjoy
574. principles of ← rationalism to admit the possibility of being wrong / ↓ that rationalist way be wrong.\
575. *The document* [BNP/E3, 15³ – 42] *was not transcribed for we consider it to be incorrectly catalogued, therefore it most likely does not pertain to the preparatory writings for the "Essay on the Nature and Meaning of Rationalism."*
576. Rat[ionalis]m
577. inf[ini]te

[44ʳ]
Rationalism[578]

The |atheist| has an attitude to what he cannot understand. That is why he easily becomes a believer, for he continues to have an attitude to what he cannot understand.

The common atheist does not believe[579] what he cannot understand — an attitude which, if consistently applied, would lead[580] almost all European materialists to a profound disbelief in the Chinese language.[581]

If most of us take astronomy on trust, that is, on authority, why not take faith on authority? Why believe in the authority of Haeckel and not in the authority of the Catholic Church? — Because astronomy has no importance and faith has.

[44ᵛ]

Apart from this, there can be no specialism in the universal.
    The one authority in God is not a theologian,[582] but God himself.

---

578. Rat[ionalis]m
579. common /↑ garden\ /↓ materialist\ atheist does not ~~be~~ ↑ believe
580. ~~give~~ ↑ lead
581. ↑ ~~existence of~~ Chinese language
582. theolog↓ian

I can trust Haeckel on astronomy because he is an astronomer and I am not; he differs from me before science.[583] (Perhaps if I were an astronomer I might not trust him.) But I cannot accept the Pope's opinion on God because he[584] does not differ from me before God.

My belief in God or not may affect my life very seriously; it[585] affects very seriously, through actions of mine derived from that belief,[586] the lives & the happiness of others. My belief or disbelief in the more or less sphericity of the earth is a variously unimportant matter.

[45ʳ]

Pascal said we must bet. If he is reincarnated somewhere about, he may take my answer: God has prohibited nothing. He has forbidden it by the statement[587] of reason, which means the ability not to decide.[588]

[133F – 64 – 64a]
Rationalism[589]

Comparison of reasoner from a central faith with the reasoning of the paranoiac.

---

583. not; ↑ he differs from me before science.
584. ~~the~~ he
585. ~~my des~~ ↑ it
586. that |belief| ↓ it
587. ↑ the statement
588. |ability| not to decide. /↓ faculty of not deciding.\
589. Rat[ionalis]m

Common sense, uncommon sense, and |non-sense.|[590]
I hold, indeed, no belief[591] for the man in the street. I am the man in the street.

That 3 are 1 is no |*mathematics|, though it may be true. Just another † = I am finally, but not in another way, when there are 3 numbers.

[64A]

You may call that good analogy, but you cannot call it automatic at all.

You may say that[592] the doctrine of the Trinity is true; you cannot say it is rational.

If it appeals to common sense, which is automatic, it is such by a simple statement thus.

— *Pode,*[593] *sim; trez pode ser um.*
— *Como?*
— *3 terços.*[594]

---

590. |non non-sense.|
591. I hold, indeed, no ↑Do I |*have transverse| any belief
592. ↑say that
593. [Ha|Pode]
594. Translation:
 — Yes, it can; three can be one.
 — How?
 — Three thirds.

An Examination of Rationalism — I.2

[15⁴ – 70 – 72]

An Examination of Rationalism

Before we can accept Reason as a criterion of knowledge, or as the only criterion of knowledge, it is legitimate that we inquire what knowledge is, and if it necessarily involves Reason, or only Reason, as its Criterion. And if it be advanced that the very idea of knowledge seems to involve that of Reason, knowledge being a rational idea, a flat contradiction may be given, seeing that knowledge in whatever it may particularly consist, is undoubtedly, in its most abstract reality, a relation between subject and object.

Knowledge involves a double relation — the exact relation to the subject of the relations among objects, or, |better|, the exact reflection in the subject of relations among objects.

It will be asked why,[595] if Reason is insufficient to be[596] a criterion of knowledge, is it sufficient[597] as a measure of the theory of knowledge; or, to revert [70ᵛ] to the old critique of scepticism, how can reason, by which alone we prove anything, prove itself irrational? The point, the conscious point, is not how it can, but that it does; and that is how sceptics, had they thought of it, would excellently have met the objection.

---

595. be ~~said that~~ ↑ asked why
596. ~~examine~~ ↑ be
597. ~~it cannot why~~ is it sufficient

The function of reason is to draw conclusions from facts; not to exist independently. Only when we examine knowledge itself can reason criticise itself, because then it is its own object, the very *fact* on which it has to prove, which it has to draw conclusions from.

Because it is only reason that criticises, Reason can criticise itself. If, criticising itself, it finds itself weak, it is not as *subject* that it is weak, but as *object*; it is not as criterion, but as sole criterion that it is weak; it is not as subject, but as object, that it fails.

When we consider life, as a testimony for matter, we consider a *fact*; and life is a fact, because[598] *we cannot explain it without destroying it.*

[71ʳ]

The only media of knowledge are the senses; reason can but coordinate the data of the senses — comparing, rendering, separating. *But it cannot destroy the data of one sense, passing it over to another.* It may reduce the apparent fact that the sun goes round the earth to the real fact that it is the earth that goes round the sun; but it does not take the fact out of the *visual sphere*. But when we seek to reduce the mental to the cerebral, we do this and we reduce an[599] order of facts sensed in one way to an order of facts sensed in another way. It is this that is illegitimate.

---

598. ∴ [because]
599. ~~one~~ an

All knowledge does indeed come from the senses. The great question is: how many senses are there?

The usual five senses are senses in relation with one kind of world — the one called physical.

Beyond these there is[600] at least one sense: the sense of the abstract. — All that is pretendedly proved as to some abstract ideas arrive presupposes, in the presupposed possibility of these being a passage to abstract ideas, the existence of these ideas. To step from step number 1 to step number 2 is easy to explain by the mechanism of stepping, but it cannot step on step number 2 unless it exists. My [71ᵛ] stepping does not create it. An abstract idea, however it may exist, is not a concrete one; that is the important point. It may be easily[601] explainable how from several tables I draw the general idea of table; but if it is explained[602] whence I draw the basis for the generalization, it is[603] not explained whence I draw the possibility of generalizing, i.e., the idea of the "general" implicit in generalizing. The question whether abstract ideas are or are not anterior is any way (in time, cause, or reason) to concrete ones is at present put beside the point; the point is only that abstract ideas are not concrete ones, i.e., otherwise put,[604] that an idea of the general is not an idea of the concrete.

---

600. ~~are~~ is
601. ↑be easily
602. ~~not~~ explained
603. ~~when~~ ↑it is
604. other↑wise ~~way~~ put

An example will render this clear. But we must not forget that, in the example, we are limiting ourselves to forms of the concrete world. When an electric motor gets a machine moving, electricity is converted into motion; the electricity that is element becomes motion, & is electricity no longer. The motion was "originated" indeed in electricity, but it is nothing like electricity; it has totally different[605] effects, manifest ones.

[72ʳ]

Are these 2 senses however — that of the abstract and that of the concrete — the only 2 senses that we have? Let us analyse these facts, and whether they will [or will] not yield further conclusions.

The concrete phenomena[606] which we presume through the medium of our five physical senses[607] are reduced by scientific investigation to one common phenomenon — vibration. Let us choose one type of these phenomena for a greater clearness. We will take light. This phenomenon which to our sense of sight exists as a concrete thing, is, for the scientists, fundamentally a mere vibration of the same[608] kind of material thing (a concrete substance — concrete because[609] it is not ab-

---

605. diff[eren]t
606. The ↑concrete phenomena
607. ↑physical senses
608. of ~~wh~~ same
609. ~~it is not~~ concrete ∴ [because]

stract) |called| "aether." [610] Now we have here a relation of a concrete fact with a concrete fact of another type. The vibration produces light when affecting our sense of light. But what sense does it affect when it is considered simply as vibration? It is not a concrete sense — sight, for instance, the only one |possible| — because[611] not only does it not affect sight, but it cannot be considered as so doing, for no imaginable microscope can show the abstract, which is such in its effects, not in its *essence*. But it is not abstract. By this neither abstract nor concrete, yet being something, we find it must appeal to some sense not abstract, nor concrete. Perhaps, if it did not appeal to the senses, we could not even imagine it. (Does not [the sense] imagine it by a trick of a small sight?) It is not motion in the concrete, because[612] that is sensible motion; it is not motion in the abstract, because[613] that is the idea of motion. What is it then?

The first fact about it is that it lies, by nature, between the concrete and the abstract. It has the characteristics of neither, though seeing, when considered in relation to the abstract to be concrete and abstract when considered in reference to the concrete.[614]

---

610. for "aether."
611. ∴ [because]
612. ∴ [because] that
613. ∴ [because]
614. the abst concrete.

[72ᵛ]

For what is it that characterizes the concrete object? Three things do: (a) the fact that it changes (in aspect?);[615] (b) the fact that it is not equal in anything to any other concrete objects of its type (other than of others it cannot be composed, as a sound neither a light as a colour); and (c) the fact that it is held to be what we are forced to call "exterior" — that is to say, outside not only our consciousness of it, but also ☐. These facts linked distinguish abstract objects (or ideas), contrasted through the five concrete ones: (a) they never change; (b) they are not comparable with one another; (c) they are not considered exterior in the sense that concrete things are.

Now the notion[616] which science points as fundamental in material manifestations exhibits characteristics both different from the two groups and intermediate to them. This essential notion (a) does not change in "appearance," but it does change, and then changes are known to us through their effects, in the concrete objects; (b) does[617] not compare except with itself and vary except in itself; (c) it is necessarily considered as spatial, though also necessarily considered undimensional — it comprises space without size [ex.].

---

615. changes ↓ (in aspect?)
616. the ~~not~~ notion
617. ~~it~~ does

Further Writings concerning Free-Will —2
Against the Death Penalty —2.1

[55 E – 2 e 3]

I.

(Free-Will)

Free-will is defined as the liberty of man to choose between a good action and a bad. Man, say the indeterminists, is either good or bad; now good, now bad.

We have first to speak of free-will itself, and to determine whether or not it exists.

The human soul is either simple or composed, that is to say, it has unity or it has not. Now, whichever of these hypotheses we accept, free-will is inconsistent with either.

If [618] the soul be simple, etc.

If composed ☐.

Let us first consider what are the arguments for free-will and what are the arguments against.

1.

Against the Death-Penalty

The principle of the death penalty, and of much incarceration, rests on 2 bases: responsibility and state rights,

---

618. ~~Since~~ If

CONCERNING FREE-WILL | AGAINST THE DEATH PENALTY

that is to say on the ultimate principle of free-will[619] and power.

Free-will[620] is an illusion; □ power is a theft. We shall proceed to prove at length these two theories and to establish their entire untruth. (Were I to[621] appeal to the benevolence of the English public, I should be acting stupidly; were[622] I to demonstrate emotionally with the state, I should be acting[623] like a madman. It is old and established that benevolence and pity are not essentials of government, that they are indeed impediments of efficient rule this is wrong.)[624]

---

619. on ↑ the ultimate principle of free-will
620. Free
    Free-will
621. two bases theories and to establish their entire untruth. (Were we ↑I to
622. we I [w|sh]ould be acting stupidly; to the were
623. I [w|sh]ould ↑ be acting
624. ↑ that they are indeed impediments of efficient rule ↓ this is wrong.
    [2ᵛ]
    Schopenhauer: "On Free-Will."
    Mill: "Examination of Hamilton's Philosophy."
    Sully: "Human Mind."
    Jonathan Edwards:
    Against.
    Contributions to the subject:
    Hobbes.
    Priestley.
    Hume.
    The Mills   Jas. Mill
                 J.S. Mill
    Bain.
    Fouillée: "Liberté et déterminisme."

161

[3ʳ]

It may occur to the reader that I am writing an emotional pamphlet, a tearful appeal to power. I am to do nothing of the sort. It is my intention to attack the death penalty philosophically, to strike at its very foundation.

The Englishmen, practical man, will at once assert that there is no need of this — that this is useless. Philosophy, he tells me, has [625] nothing to do with practice. What we want, he added, is common sense.

But the popular idea of philosophy is very [626] extraordinary, and, like all popular ideas, very wrong.

Free will contrary to the idea of Law.

It is not enough that monarchy, aristocracy, religion contrary to all truth, be still among us. We have yet war, and the brutal and unsparing temperament of the English race has preserved among them the death penalty. It is of this that I must speak. I write with hope of a hearing, though sooner will the stud forsake this desert [627] than the English race will drop the many vestiges of lowness and of brutality which endeavours & determines [628] to keep and which are, in the saying of Englishmen, in the very strangled and moral walls of the nation. For my part I had wished the English people had better [629] moral support than religion, convention and power.

---

625. me, ~~is~~ has
626. philosophy ᵥ is very
627. the ~~and~~ ↑ stud forsake ~~the~~ ↑ this desert
628. endeavours ↑ and determines
629. ~~aron~~ ↑ better

An English's [630] house is his castle; and convention, prejudice, moral cowardice, which we may express by one word — conservatism — are the walls and structure thereof. [631]

2.2 — Essay on Liberty

Project

[48H – 61]

Plan of an Essay on Liberty. Or on [the] Basis of Ethics. [632]

I. The Moral Law
   (3 rules). (Ethics in regard to the individual.)

   Other rules of liberty [633]

(1) Equal for all men; each man's liberty ends where another's begins.
(2) A man must have the liberty he gives.

(Death-penalty: cannot be applied because against *moral laws*.) [634]

---

630. E[nglish]'s
631. structure ~~of the Briton's home~~ ↑ thereof
632. Plan of an Essay on Liberty. → Or on the Basis of Ethics.
633. † liberty
634. ∴ [because] against *moral laws*.[)]

[61ᵛ]

Rights of the Individual

(1) Liberty

Individual rights of the individual.
Social rights of the individual.[635]
Super-social rights of the individual.[636]

primarily

That of living   That of the *sans* pain   That of attaining
                                           his development

Right to think   Then

Crimes Against —

Individual purely: 1. murder 2. oppression (even if it causes? no pain)

Society: 1. □

General[637] humanity: 1. Keeping or coming in[638] ignorance and in immorality.

---

635. indiv[idual].
636. indiv[idual].
637. General /↑ super-†\
638. Keeping ↑ or coming in

Fragments
[15¹ – 38ʳ]

By liberty is understood the Power of doing either good or evil; therefore the act of doing neither good nor evil, therefore superiority to good and to evil. — Free-will is not a thing of this world. —

Do all men partake of free-will as they partake of life, equally, in⁶³⁹ a way mysteriously equal.

[15¹ – 48]

Idea of good — source of action, origin of the idea of Free-Will.⁶⁴⁰

The⁶⁴¹ idea of liberty comes from the consciousness of two opposite impulses, one of⁶⁴² good, another of evil.

---

639. ~~m~~ ↑in
640. F[ree]-Will.
641. ~~The~~ The
642. ↑one of

[15⁵ – 23]⁶⁴³

[23ᵛ]

In Free-will⁶⁴⁴ I do not believe. But free-will is one thing and moral⁶⁴⁵ liberty another. I am determined to be what I am, to be personally⁶⁴⁶ free or a slave; free-will does not exist. But in my slavery there are degrees of a secondly liberty, personal, or moral liberty.

L'universel doit être supérieur, non contraire au Moi. (Here not mystic altruism).

[15A – 83 e 84]

How⁶⁴⁷ are deductions false? How are accepted ideas

---

643. [23ʳ]
    Genius an activity of liberation.
    Est libre tout ce qui agit en vue de l'universel. Si j'agis en vue de ma faim, de mon désir, de □, je ne suis pas libre. Et c'est par lui que la vertu est grande, puisqu'elle agit en vue du bien universel. Le génie s'il chant que ce qui est mauvais, presque libre par cela qu'il cherche, dans l'art, la beauté, n'est pas libre dans ce qu'il ne cherche pas le bien.
    La plus grande liberté que l'un peut avoir (au monde) est la liberté de l'homme de bien.
    Over
644. ~~Men d~~
    In Free-Will
645. moral /↑ personal\
646. ~~see~~ be personally
647. *Max Vernon*: ["]Psycho-physiological studies of the Protists."
    How far has science a hold upon metaphysics? How far can science contradict and correct ~~this~~ the most ~~central~~ ↑ general science of all.

false? How, in the course[648] of nature, where all is of course natural, is there a place for error? How is error possible?

[83ᵛ]

The *encouraging* effect of pride. Pombal[649] or Chateaubriand.

Is there anything analogous to the transmutation of the idea of physical liberty into the idea of moral liberty? Any other argument from the physical into the moral world?

Influence of the human idea of good on the idea of moral liberty.

What is the mental difference between man and the higher animals? The intellect differs only in degree. All the difference[650] is in the idea of good, idea of *benevolence*,

---

Albrecht Rau: "Sensation and Thought."
Haeckel: "Anthropogeny." (Evolution of Man).
Oken and *Neckel*: (1806) "On the Alimentary Canal."
Carl Ernst Baer. ↓ 1828 "History of the Development of Animal: Observations and Reflections."

Haeckel: "Natural History of Creation."

~~Psycho Natural Haeckel~~ Idea of liberty

648. the ~~whole~~ course
649. Marquis de Pombal (1699–1782) was Secretary of the State during the reign of King José I of Portugal, and the *Algarves* under Joseph I of Portugal from 1750–1777. He had a significant role in the reconstruction of Lisbon after the earthquake in 1755.
650. diff[eren]ce

idea of altruism. By this idea man learns what the animals cannot know, to be against nature, & in contradiction with some of its laws.

The difference between the savage of Tierra del Fuego, who has no idea of good, [84ʳ] no idea of justice, no notion of altruism, the difference between this poor creature and the higher apes is smaller than his[651] difference from such a type of manhood as was represented in Christ.[652]

How did the idea of good, non-natural idea appear? Is it not strange that, at a certain point of evolution, an idea entirely heterogeneous □.

Notes on Haeckel

Gastrea Theory — unicellular or loose multicellular —

I. Animals[653] are divided into Protozoa (non-tissued) and Metazoa (tissued).

II. Protozoa[654] multiply, usually, non-sexually. Metazoa[655] generally propagate sexually.

III. □

---

651. than ~~the d~~ his
652. was /↑ is\ represented in /↑ by\ Christ
653. *Gastrea Theory* → – unicellular or loose multicellular – I. [~~These~~|Animals]
654. Pr[otozo]a
655. Met[azo]a

3 — Fragments with References to the Idea of Cause

[22 – 96]

Psychological Automatism

Automatic motion (*sans* consciousness in the whole individual) of an arm[656] is the effect of a cause — will in the cells, molecules, or etc., which constitutes that arm.

CRA

What is double personality?

?

Every spiritual act has the character of absoluteness or of infinity. Thought is neither extended nor temporal. It is the sensation of that thought which is in time and in space.

"To say judgment, reasoning, etc. is but the displacement of molecules[657] is to talk nonsense. The *phainomena* are none the less heterogeneous."

[96ᵛ]

Definition of cause (Schopenhauer): "The antecedent modification which renders necessary the consequent modification."

---

656. arm ~~ea~~
657. ~~certain~~ molecules

(Scholastic): "*Per causam intelligo id quo sublato tollitur effectus.*" This last definition has[658] the defect of being also applicable to the conditions of a fact (*phainomenon*).

Cf. taking away space and time.

Definition: "By *necessary* is understood all that results from a given sufficient reason."

"The Ego," says Taine, "is but a property common to all the phenomena of consciousness, the property that they have of appearing to us as interior, abstracted from phenomena and transformed by words into substance."

Is this not an argument similar to the Idea-argument of Plato?

CRA

[23 – 28]

Difference between Causation, excitation, and motivation, to use the terms of Schopenhauer:

Causation is, for instance, in us, in the movement along the nerves; excitation in the alteration these make; and motivation in the action born of the excitation.

Thus excitation is the change of a movement of transference[659] to a movement of alteration. Motivation appears to be the passing of a movement of alteration into a movement of transference.

---

658. last ↑ definition has
659. mov[emen]t of transferrence

But what is a movement of alteration? Is it ideal? It is natural[660] that anything occupying time should alter, and that all things in space should be in movement; these things are contained in the nature of the notions [of] time and of space.

[28ᵛ]

How can this be by the side of the theory that *excitation* is the *emotion*, which is of the nature of *idea-thing*?

Everything is bound to be in time and in space, since these ideas exist. Therefore there cannot be any movement[661] of alteration only; it must be accompanied by some movement[662] of transference. Now, movement of transference is of 2 kinds: movement of continuation and movement of vibration, that is to say, movement without return and movement[663] with return. Alteration itself is not material, it is a purely ideal phenomenon; the material correspondent is a movement of some kind. § The question then is made simpler; it becomes a question of transmission of movement purely of transference, all in the material plane.

---

660. is ~~normal and~~ natural
661. mov[emen]t
662. mov[emen]t
663. mov[emen]t of transference is of 2 kinds: mov[emen]t of continuation and mov[emen]t of vibration, that is to say, mov[emen]t ~~of~~ without return and mov[emen]t

From the Notebook of Charles Robert Anon

[13A – 5a – 4a]

1. Cause is anterior and external to effect.
2. Whence, Cause & Effect must be in, and cannot be out of Space and Time.
3. Cause & Effect are of the same nature. (Being things in Space and in time.)
4. ☐

"On the Idea of Cause"
 Les amateurs de l'Inutile
 "*La pénultième est morte.*"

[5aᵛ]

Cause and Effect are two phenomena so concrete that we cannot define one completely without[664] defining the other. In this they differ from 2 any successive phenomena such as night and day. *Ay.* Why do we not consider night and day as effect and cause?

N. the confusion often made between Cause and Conditions. The ground a house stands on is one of the conditions of that house. It is not its Cause. Similarly the mortar, the hikes, the wood. None of these are causes; yet all are needed — without them the house were not. Hence the defect of the scholastic definition of cause: *id quo ablato tollitur effectus.*

---

664. one ↑completely without

"For instance the night succeeds the day and the day the night but we call not the day [665] [the] cause of the night, nor the night [the] cause of the Day."

Cause = originating power. Seems true and the reason why we say not the day causes the night & the night the day. Or is it because they occupy the same space, one after another? Because they do not represent a movement but a substitution?

Cause is a succession in movement? For instance [666] a man, in football, kicking a ball. The cause of the movement [667] of the ball is the energy [668] in the muscles of the man; the cause of this is the message (also a movement) sent from the brain; and this communication is the effect of the vibration [669] of the optic nerve consequent on the observation of the how the ball was moving. Is there here any idea of Cause, any real idea, be it understood? Or is this but a species of motion?

[4a^v]

If an "external" reality be the Cause of our sensation, then, according to the 3rd law of cause, it must be of the same nature as the effect. Then [670] since we know all by sensation, sensation is reality. For, otherwise, the Cause

---

665. ~~night~~ day
666. For ~~a~~ instance
667. The ~~effect~~ cause of the mov[emen]t
668. ~~mov~~ energy
669. vibration /↑ movement and cells vibrating\
670. ~~But to suppose an extrernal object is represented~~ Then

would reproduce itself in our brain and we should perceive nothing greater than that.

Reply: We perceive a movement, which, no matter [the] size,[671] is always a movement.

Fragments with References to the Concept of Sensation — 4

[15³ – 26]

Diminution of the sensation of *arrêt*.[672]

Notion of space, for Haeckel,[673] results from an association between the states of consciousness.

Desire is the predominance of a representation which fights against the obstacles and *par lui*[674] determines in this sense other representations.

p. 70 (Ribot)[675] Lotze (passage from)[676]

---

671. size /↑ scope\
672. sens[ation] of *arrêt*
673. H[aeckel],
674. *Originally in French.*
675. Théodule-Armand Ribot (1839–1916) was a French psychologist who followed the experimental method in psychology. His works are influenced by the sensationalist school. There is a reference in Alexander Search's reading notebook to nine of Ribot's works [BNP/E3, 144H – 28ʳ eᵛ]: *Les maladies de la mémoire; Les maladies de la volonté; Les maladies de la personnalité; Psychologie de l'attention; Essai sur l'imagination créatrice; L'hérédité. Étude psychologique; La psychologie des sentiments; L'évolution des idées générales; La logique des sentiments.*

Intensive sensations
Extensive sensations
Sensation grows as the logarithm [677] of the excitation.
Sensation grows as the logarithm of the excitation.

[25 – 78r]

There are no past sensations. Memory is a sensation of a sensation. Sensation is always present.
(The world is an infinity of presents.)
Similarly prevision is a sensation of a sensation also — future.

[15B² – 33]

On Binet's [678] Proof of the World's Existence

Sensations [679] suppose a nervous system, a nervous system a body, a body a space, etc.
Answer.
Sensation dividing itself into subject and object, returns to itself, materialized, localized; thus [680] the body is sensationed, and conceived as sensing.

---

676. Rudolf Hermann Lotze (1817–1881) was a German philosopher who defended the existence of a mind of the world that rules the mechanical laws of the universe.
677. log[arithm]
678. ↑*On Binet's*
679. A̶ Sensations
680. f̶o̶r̶ thus

What is the nature of the atom? Infinite divisibility of matter. Is the atom divisible? At least inessentially?

[33ᵛ]

Whatever is extended is divisible; if not, what then. The atom must be extended; if extended divisible, and, within itself, *ad infinitum*. If it be indivisible it is unextended; and if unextended, there is no matter because a number, however large, of unextended things cannot make anything extended.

AFTERWORD

This edition of Pessoa's *Philosophical Essays* is an excellent and timely contribution to the greater cultural visibility of an author, who, in spite of being already hailed worldwide as a poetic & literary genius, is not yet fully recognized for the fecundity of his philosophical works. The present work has the merit of contextualizing the philosophical fragments in relation to the original projects conceived by Pessoa, texts that have previously been published only piecemeal, in random and diffuse — if not confusing — ways. It also has the merit of presenting a substantial body of unpublished texts of Pessoa's English pre-heteronyms that appeared early in his "drama in people," enabling a greater understanding of the roots of Pessoa's inquietude, interrogation, and philosophical conception. It also contributes to a deeper understanding of the true importance of his self-designation as "a poet animated by philosophy." If the texts published in this edition allow the discovery of some of the most important roots of the philosophical dimension of Pessoa's work, these roots in return are brought to fruition in the totality of his work. Pessoa's work is an enigma, representing a chaotic cosmos, a *chaosmos*, of *incompossible* ideas and his philosophical interests should not be taken as a promise of systematic consistency.

Pessoa is a paradoxical thinker who lives the radical experience of having no personality and of being nobody whilst discovering at the heart of this experience the possibility of "imagining himself everything" and of "being" and "feeling everything in everyway," inhabiting each moment "in a successive and diverse internal world," as one reads in a passage concerning Omar Khayyám quoted in the introduction to this edition. Although, in the fictional essay that was his entire life, Pessoa had played the game of the creation of aesthetic and philosophical movements, he didn't create the thought of a thinker determined by one personality, nor even of a systematic thinker. His philosophical thoughts in fact belong to other multiple personalities who think, feel, and live everything in limited, discontinuous, and changeable perspectives. His sense of horror before the definite, and his rejection of the beginning and the end of everything evade any label. On the contrary, it offers only random glimpses of uncoordinated and unarticulated visions, gaps in a labyrinth that no one goes through, curves of a way that doesn't exist, because, like a hiker, it escapes all the ways and positions, as Pessoa's fictional personality Raphael Baldaya expresses magnificently in "The Way of the Serpent."

---

1. Cf. Paulo Borges, *O teatro da vacuidade ou a impossibilidade de ser eu. Estudos e ensaios pessoanos* (Lisbon: Verbo/Babel, 2011); also the forthcoming *Il teatro della vacuità o l'impossibilità di essere io. Studi e saggi pessoani* (Milan: Bietti, 2013).

The "Theatre of the Vacuity" offers an empty stage to be filled and saturated by the author's dramatic multitude, for the "impossibility of being a self"[1] is the bottomless bottom of one's inner panpsychism, where each criticized philosophy is one embodied soul, where there's always place for one more ebullition of the possible, constituting a (not-)subject that is a multitude of the thinkable, that is, constituting the unthinkable character of this, the not-being of every being, the empty of all the complete, the "King of Gaps," who is the "lord of what is twixt thing and thing, / of interbeings."[2] In this way, this (not-)subject shelters in itself "thousands of philosophies" that don't agree with one another, "thousands of theories" on the world, on man, and on all the problems that pertain to metaphysics; theories that are both extraordinary and profound, theories that were never written and soon vanished, as forgotten as those dreams[3] that live on nonetheless in the secret and woodsy life of the unconscious.

The literary and philosophical work of Pessoa is an experiment toward another way of being a self and a man, a way of being that lies beyond being. It is an experiment in the mutation of the human into an over-human, revealing in ourselves that which never

---

2. Cf. Fernando Pessoa, "The King of Gaps," in *Poesia Inglesa I*, ed. and tr. by Luísa Freire (Lisbon: Assírio & Alvim, 2000) 280.

3. BNP/E3, 15B³-12.

was but can be human without being inhuman. The literary and philosophical work of Pessoa establishes, therefore, a new civilizational paradigm, fulfilling the promise of Portuguese messianism inspired by the prophet Daniel's interpretation of the dream of Nebuchadnezzar (Daniel 2:31–45). It projects us towards a "Fifth Empire," with its negative overcoming, — as in the Hegelian *Aufhebung* — of the foundational moments of the history of the world: the Greek, Roman, Christian, and European — as well as non-European — cultural models. In that integrative overcoming, philosophy also changes itself into another way of thinking, which proceeds from another thought. It now becomes an abyss without subject wherein a new and radical beginning must spring forth, and open up all possibilities.

At a time when Pessoa studies, after focusing on literary analyses, is beginning to attain a more rigorous philological approach under the impulsion of philosophical hermeneutics and of the international dissemination of Pessoa's work through the efforts of a new generation of researchers,[4] this carefully prepared and distinctive edition by Nuno Ribeiro — one of the most promising of these new researchers —,[5]

---

4. Cf. AAVV, *Olhares Europeus sobre Fernando Pessoa*, organized by Paulo Borges (Lisbon: Centro de Filosofia da Universidade de Lisboa, 2010).

5. Cf. Nuno Ribeiro, *Fernando Pessoa e Nietzsche: o pensamento da pluralidade* (Lisbon: Verbo/Babel, 2011).

with its enlightening introduction, presents to the global public fundamental texts for the comprehension and reappraisal of this cultural phenomenon, the heritage not merely of one nation but of humanity, called Fernando Pessoa.

Paulo Borges
UNIVERSITY OF LISBON
Department of Philosophy

BIBLIOGRAPHY

Alain Badiou, *Handbook of Inaesthetics* (Stanford: Stanford University Press, 2005).

Paulo Borges, *O Teatro da Vacuidade ou a impossibilidade de ser eu. Estudos e ensaios pessoanos* (Lisbon: Editora Verbo, 2011).

Paulo Borges, ed., *Olhares europeus sobre Fernando Pessoa* (Lisbon: Centro de Filosofia da Universidade de Lisbon, 2010).

Silke Buss, *Fernando Pessoa auf europäischen Bühnen* (Munster: Lit Verlag, 1999).

Steffen Dix, *Heteronymie und Neopaginismus bei Fernando Pessoa Epistemata Philosophie* (Würzburg: Verlag Königshausen & Neumann, 2005).

K. David Jackson, *Advance Genres in Fernando Pessoa* (Oxford: Oxford University Press, 2010).

Zbigniew Kotowicz, *Fernando Pessoa: Voices of a Nomadic Soul* (Bristol: Shearsman Books, 2008).

Teresa Rita Lopes, ed., *Pessoa Inédito* (Lisbon: Livros Horizonte, 1993).

Teresa Rita Lopes, *Pessoa por Conhecer, Vols. I e II* (Lisbon: Editorial Estampa, 1990).

Pablo Javier Pérez López, *Poesía, Ontología y Tragedia en Fernando Pessoa* (Madrid: Editorial Manuscritos, 2012).

George Monteiro, *The Presence of Pessoa: English, American, and Southern African Literary Responses* (Kentucky: University Press of Kentucky, 1998).

Pedro Teixeira da Mota, *Fernando Pessoa. Moral, Regras de Vida, Condições de Iniciação*, texts established and commented on by Pedro Teixeira da Mota (Lisbon: Edições Manuel Lencastre, 1988).

Fernando Pessoa, *Cadernos, Tomo I*, ed. by Jerónimo Pizarro (Lisbon: Imprensa Nacional-Casa da Moeda, 2009).

Fernando Pessoa, *Escritos Autobiográficos, Automáticos e de Reflexão Pessoal*, ed. by Richard Zenith (Lisbon: Assírio & Alvim, 2003).

Fernando Pessoa, *Escritos sobre Génio e Loucura*, vols. I and II, ed. by Jerónimo Pizarro (Lisbon: Imprensa Nacional Casa da Moeda, 2006).

Fernando Pessoa, *Páginas de Estética e de Teoria e Crítica Literárias*, texts established and commented on by Georg Lind & Jacinto do Prado Coelho (Lisbon: Ática, 1994).

Fernando Pessoa, *Textos Filosóficos de Fernando Pessoa*, established and prefaced by António Pina Coelho, Volume I e II (Lisbon: Ática, 1994).

Nuno Ribeiro & Cláudia Souza, "Charles Robert Anon & Alexander Search: Filosofia e Psiquiatria," *Revista Filosófica de Coimbra*, Nº 42 (*forthcoming*).

Nuno Ribeiro, *Fernando Pessoa e Nietzsche: O pensamento da Pluralidade* (Lisbon: Verbo, 2011).

Nuno Ribeiro, "Os Livro Filosóficos Inacabados de Pessoa — Problemas e Critérios para a Publicação dos Escritos Filosóficos de Pessoa," *Philosophica*, Nº 38 (Lisbon: Edições Colibri, 2011) 165–174.

Nuno Ribeiro, "'Tive em mim milhares de Filosofias' — queftões para a edição dos escritos filosóficos inéditos de Pessoa," *Cultura ENTRE Culturas*, Nº 3 (Lisbon: Âncora Editora, 2011) 192–200.

Nuno Ribeiro, *Tradição e Pluralismo nos Escritos Filosóficos de Fernando Pessoa / Escritos Filosóficos de Fernando Pessoa* (Lisbon: Faculdade de Ciências Sociais e Humanas da Universidade Nova de Lisbon, 2012).

Cláudia Souza, *Ciências do Psiquismo Humano, Política e Criação Literária no efpólio de Fernando Pessoa (1905–1914)* (Belo Horizonte: PUC — Minas Gerais, 2011).

COLOPHON

PHILOSOPHICAL ESSAYS was typeset in InDesign 5.0.
The text & page numbers are set in *Adobe Jenson Pro*.
The titles are set in *Monotype Gill Sans*.

Book design & typesetting: Alessandro Segalini
Cover design: István Orosz

PHILOSOPHICAL ESSAYS
is published by Contra Mundum Press
and printed by Lightning Source, which has received Chain of
Custody certification from: The Forest Stewardship Council,
The Programme for the Endorsement of Forest Certification,
and The Sustainable Forestry Initiative.

Contra Mundum Press New York

CONTRA MUNDUM PRESS

Contra Mundum Press is dedicated to the value & the indispensable importance of the individual voice.

Contra Mundum Press will be publishing titles from all the fields in which the genius of the age traditionally produces the most challenging and innovative work: poetry, novels, theatre, philosophy — including philosophy of science & of mathematics — criticism, and essays. Upcoming volumes include Richard Foreman's *Plays with Films*, Friedrich Nietzsche's *Greek Music Drama*, & Jean-Jacques Rousseau's *Narcissus*.

For the complete list of forthcoming publications, please visit our website. To be added to our mailing list, send your name and email address to: info@contramundum.net

Contra Mundum Press
P.O. Box 1326
New York, NY 10276
USA
http://contramundum.net

ACKNOWLEDGMENTS

I would like to express my gratitude to Nuno Venturinha, a specialist at the Wittgenstein Archive, kept at the University of Bergen (WAB), Norway, who persuaded me that the use of new symbols in these transcriptions would benefit Pessoa studies. I am also indebted to him for other suggestions made use of in this edition. To Claudia Souza, I express my gratitude for companionship during my numerous incursions to the Pessoa Archive, and for a number of suggestions concerning Pessoa's philosophical writings. Her remarks about Charles Robert Anon & Alexander Search also proved illuminating. Finally, I want to thank the the two anonymous readers who significantly aided my refining the introduction.

Printed in March 2021
by Rotomail Italia S.p.A., Vignate (MI) - Italy